"The author's words inspire us towards resilience and perseverance. *Under Water* stirs us to choose hope when circumstances seem hopeless, to cherish our families, and to come alongside and give generously to our suffering neighbors."

—Bunny Bennett, author of *God Thinks I'm Beautiful*

"Owen takes the reader on a perilous journey through one of [Nashville's] most difficult times. This is an account that everyone needs to read. Frankly, this book is so well written it should be recognized by Nashville's mayor Megan Barry as an official historical document."

—Bob Williams, author of *Music City Macabre*

Under Water:
A Natural Disaster Memoir

Owen Grimenstein

Dedication

Allison, you are the editor, the content, and the character developer of my life. Without you, I would be an incomplete manuscript in a forgotten drawer.

Contents

Preface

Here are the facts:

In May of 2010, Nashville, Tennessee, was hit with a storm system that resulted in a devastating flood that took the lives of twenty-six people, eighteen of whom were in Middle Tennessee,[1] and caused forty-eight counties in the state to be declared major disaster areas.[2]

The National Weather Service predicted Nashville would receive one or two inches of rain on Saturday, May 1, and another one or two inches on Sunday, May 2.[3] Instead, the official rain totals measured at the Nashville International Airport were over six inches on Saturday and had accumulated to just more than thirteen and a half inches by Sunday night. This set a new two-day record that more than doubled the previous record of 6.68 inches in 1979 in the wake of Hurricane Frederic.[4]

Other areas in Middle Tennessee accumulated a great deal more rain. Bellevue, an unincorporated area of Metro Nashville in west Davidson County, received the greatest total rainfall in the county with 17.67 inches falling in less than thirty-eight hours.[5] Fairview, a town in Williamson County west of Bellevue, recorded 18.04 inches of rain, the highest amount in Middle Tennessee during this storm system.[6] Only two days into the month, officials had already declared this the wettest May in Nashville's recorded history and the fifth wettest month in city history.[7]

The torrential rainfall in such a short period of time overwhelmed the many creeks and rivers that are part of the Middle Tennessee landscape. The Cumberland River crested at 51.86 feet, almost twelve feet above flood stage,[8] causing devastating flooding to businesses and homes in and around downtown Nashville. The Harpeth River reached its highest level at more than thirty-three feet, about nine feet above flood stage,[9] resulting in widespread flooding throughout the Middle Tennessee region. The US Army Corp of Engineers noted that this storm was far greater than a one thousand-year event for the hardest hit areas,[10] meaning that each year a storm of this magnitude has less than one-tenth of 1 percent chance of happening.[11]

In the Nashville area alone, eleven people died,[12] more than one hundred roads were closed, and hundreds of people were rescued from flood waters. At least eleven thousand structures were damaged.[13] The estimated cost to rebuild was more than two billion dollars. On Interstate 24 alone, about seventy cars were submerged. This was named the costliest disaster in Nashville's history[14] and the fourth largest non-hurricane disaster in US history.[15]

Following the disaster, many Middle Tennesseans were upset that this flood seemed to get very little national attention. The news coverage that weekend focused on a foiled bomb scare in New York City and a burning BP oil rig in the Gulf of Mexico that killed eleven people and resulted in a devastating oil spill. Many journalists and bloggers speculated in their articles that Nashville did not get the media attention because the city's people quickly stepped up to help one another. Instead of looting and violence, neighbors fed one another and shared resources and time. They helped one another rebuild their homes and their lives.

Unlike most articles, blogs, and books that have been written about the flood, I did not want to talk in detail about how the flood affected the city as a whole or about the amazing spirit of a city that could have broken down but chose not to. Though these are important topics to discuss, I wanted to document one man's journey through a natural disaster. I wanted to focus on one perspective among the thousands that will never be told. This is my story.

I.

It Was Our Home

"Rain fell on Nashville for more than thirty-six hours straight—an amount of rain our city had never seen in its recorded history."

— State of Metro Address
by Mayor Karl Dean
May 1, 2012

1

An Unlikely Rain

Saturday, May 1, 2010, was exactly two years to the day after my wife and I purchased our home on Beech Bend Drive in Nashville, Tennessee. We had nothing special planned to commemorate this, of course, but commented on how we couldn't believe that we had already lived there for two years. Otherwise, it was just a typical, but rainy, day. We would have approached things differently had we known that this day was going to become an important anniversary of a different kind. This day was going to mark the beginning of a new journey.

There were three main storm systems that came through very close together in the days leading up to May 1. Allison, my wife of five years, and I had been watching the weather reports, and every time it looked like the end of the rain was near, another system would show up on the radar. We had never seen so much rain. It wasn't just moving through the region; the massive reds and greens on the radars were developing in our section of town over and over again.

Though other areas were getting severe storms and tornadoes, I don't remember getting a lot of lightning or wind despite all the fuss from the media about the severity expected. We may have gotten some of these severe storms, but all that stood out to me at the time was the duration and sheer quantity of rain.

Country music star Brad Paisley, who owns property near Nashville, described the rain perfectly when he said, "It came down harder than I've ever seen it rain here. You know how when you're in a mall and it's coming down in sheets, and you think, I'll give it five minutes, and when it lets up I'll run to my car? Well, imagine that it didn't let up until the next day."[16]

3:10 p.m. After raining most of the day, the first river Flood Warning" was issued for the Harpeth River in Bellevue. Neither Allison nor I ever remember seeing this warning before. It still didn't seem to be that relevant to us, however. I thought about the people who were living in low-lying areas and how it might impact them. I went ahead and proceeded with the plans I had for that day, assuming we wouldn't be affected.

I recently had finished rebuilding our backyard deck and had a lot of old wood that I needed to dispose of before my son, Patrick's, first birthday party in a week, so I borrowed my dad's truck to haul it off. On my way to Fairview to return the truck to my parents, I noticed ditches full of water and creeks along the road were full and flowing rapidly.

In a few places, I noticed that the moving water was level with the road and close to flowing over. This was the case just before I got to the seafoam-colored bridge on Highway 100 close to Highway 96 in Nashville, where water had already gotten high enough that it was beginning to overtake the road. It was just an inch or two deep, but it wasn't just an inch or two of standing water that you would see in a heavy downpour. This wasn't just a puddle; this part of the road was now under the Harpeth River.

When I drove over the bridge, the water was so high it looked like it was almost touching the underside of the bridge. It was moving quickly and reminded me of the white water rapids of the Ocoee River that I rafted on as a teenager. I wondered about the integrity of the bridge. Immediately after I passed the bridge I saw men trying to pull their white pickup truck and some heavy construction equipment out of the flooded parking lot of a small business that sits on one side of the road. The truck was submerged halfway up its open driver's side window.

I made it out to my parents' and told them what I had seen. My mom was a little concerned and offered for me to stay at their house if I needed to. I was anxious to get home though, so I exchanged my dad's truck for my car and started driving back to Bellevue.

As I approached the same green bridge I'd driven over less than thirty minutes earlier, I saw a fire truck blocking the road on the far side of the bridge. On my side of the bridge, some people had parked and gotten out of their cars, alerting oncoming drivers to turn around. Had these people not stopped and redirected traffic, someone could have gotten hurt or killed by the water that was now rushing over the road.

I turned around in front of the little business where earlier I'd seen the men trying to save the truck, now feeling a true sense of danger. The seriousness of the situation was starting to sink in, not necessarily for my personal safety but for other people. Rubbernecking and sight-seeing were no longer priorities. I didn't even think to look behind the business to see if they'd gotten the truck out. My focus was on getting home.

I turned onto Highway 96, two-tenths of a mile from the spot that was now flooding. Less than a mile later, traffic was stopped on another little bridge; people were slowly driving through the gushing water that was flooding the road just past the bridge, about a foot deep and maybe thirty yards wide. I waited in the stop-and-go traffic until I was almost to the front of the line. Pulling over to the shoulder of the bridge, just feet from the water, I watched people slowly drive past me and cross with no problems.

As I looked at the property off the left side of the road, I was briefly in awe of the volume of water flowing through it. The land was much lower than the road, so the water was deep, and there were very few trees or structures—just an empty field. The house that sat on this field was at the back of the property on elevated land and seemed to be out of immediate danger. I imagined being in that house watching my front yard turn into a lake, fearful of the slowly approaching water.

With no ground to provide traction and no trees to get caught in, the river would take total control of any vehicle swept into it. The occupants of the car would have to ride it out until it washed up downriver or until the person driving the car evacuated to fend for himself against the rushing current.

I could feel the bridge and my car shaking from the force of the water flowing beneath it, which was so high it was touching and pushing against the bottom of the bridge. Water was splashing up like waves against cliffside rocks.

I felt as secure sitting on that bridge as I would be attempting to cross through the water covering the road. At any moment, I expected the bridge to give out and I'd scramble just to keep myself above water like an ant on a floating stick.

All I could think about was all of the news channels that tell you over and over never to cross the water on a road because you don't know how strong the current is or what may be underneath it. Suddenly their catchphrase, "Turn around, don't drown" didn't seem so silly. I've always just rolled my eyes at that advice. It was common sense; only an idiot would try to cross a flooded road. They also say it only takes eight to twelve inches of water to sweep a car away. The water on the road was in that range and maybe more in the middle. The road could have been washing away for all I knew. I sat there on the shoulder of the bridge and watched several people pass over the bridge and into the flooded road without incident. I thought about turning around and going back to Fairview to stay with my parents, but I felt the need to get back to Patrick and Allison.

2

Together

I married my beautiful best friend, Allison, in 2005. We both grew up in Tennessee with a two-and-a-half-hour drive separating us; she in Memphis and I in Fairview. When I was playing soccer, she was dancing ballet. I played with G.I. Joe and rode my bike through the hilly country roads while she played with dolls and rode her bike on suburban streets. While she was studying hard in school, I was trying not to.

I graduated high school and took the thirty-minute journey to Nashville to attend Lipscomb University, a private, Christian school my family had strong ties to: my parents and sister attended, my grandfather taught Chemistry there for thirty years, and my grandmother worked in the bookstore for many years. My childhood friend Joe Christy was a year ahead of me and also went to Lipscomb. I was able to room with him for the couple of years we attended together. He helped motivate me to study and I soon received a business degree.

After graduating high school with honors, Allison moved across the state to attend the University of Tennessee, Knoxville. She worked toward a psychology degree at the alma mater of many of her family members. This degree eventually led her to a master's degree and career in social work.

We had no way of knowing each other and even less reason to meet. I could tell you about the stars aligning and claim that the butterfly effect is what brought us to each other. I don't know if a cicada sneezed in Cameroon, which caused a small breeze, followed by a gust of wind over the Atlantic Ocean, and a barometric pressure change over Tennessee that resulted in an impulsive last-second decision that caused us to run in to each other. But I believe God intervenes sometimes when we aren't aware of it. Any of these scenarios may or may not have been the case. One thing I am sure about is that I was the luckiest guy on earth the night I met her.

In October 2002, we were both well into our college lives when Allison decided to stop by Nashville on her way home for fall break. She had a friend she grew up dancing with who lived on the first floor of an apartment building next to Belmont University. This was the first time she had seen her in a while and thought it would be nice to break up the long drive across Tennessee. Plus, her friend happened to mention that there were three "cute soccer guys" that lived in the apartment above her.

On the night Allison arrived in Nashville, my friends and I had just played an indoor soccer game. We lost but were pumped up because we had played well against several players who played for the local semi-pro league.

We got back to our apartment and saw that our downstairs neighbor was having a party. We knew her well enough to go check it out. So, down we went, still dressed in our sweaty soccer gear.

As soon as I walked in the door I saw Allison. I think I walked around the apartment and talked to others for a few minutes, but I soon returned to the living room and sat on the floor between Allison and another girl. The girl sitting on my right had been drinking and was clearly interested in talking with me, but I couldn't help but keep my focus on the girl to my left. Allison captivated me.

I can't tell you the first words we spoke to each other but I do know that she held her own while talking about sports. I teased her after she told me that she was a Detroit Red Wings fan and that her team won the Stanley Cup the year before, telling her that she was mistaken because they'd won two years before, and we went back and forth like this for a while. She was right of course; that is just how I must have decided to flirt.

Aware that I was still in my soccer gear and probably didn't smell the way I would have liked when meeting a pretty girl for the first time, I excused myself to go upstairs to shower and change. I was worried she would move on or leave early, but I had to change if I was going to continue "wooing" her.

She apparently was thinking the same thing; I might not return if she didn't do something. So before I left she said, "You know who you look like?" I assumed that she was going to say James Van Der Beek, the actor on *Dawson's Creek* and whose character precipitated my nickname, Dawson. Although he's an attractive guy, she wasn't going to impress me with that. I playfully pretended I didn't want to hear it and continued to go outside. I was halfway up the stairs when she leaned her head outside the door and said, "I was going to say Edward Norton!" Now we were in business.

I took the quickest shower I had ever taken and returned to the party. What would come after that night would be our very own romantic comedy, filled with lots of laughs, emotional ups and downs (mostly ups), and too many cheesy one-liners to count. That night we wrote the first lines in the book of our future.

3

A Dangerous Decision

4:36 p.m. Still sitting on the bridge, I decided to cross the flooded road. It was one of those moments when you know you shouldn't do something, but your mind talks you into it anyway. I called Allison and told her what was going on, leaving out the part about how high the water was, and made sure I told her that I loved her in a way that wouldn't throw up any red flags. I turned on my blinker and a lady in a blue minivan let me pull out in front of her. Within seconds, I was on the road, driving through water.

I immediately regretted doing it but knew it was too late to stop. I unbuckled my seatbelt and rolled down my window so that if my car got swept away and submerged I could easily escape. The closer I got to the center of the newly-created river, the deeper it got. At one point the water was higher than the bottom of my door. I wanted to look down to make sure the murky water wasn't coming in, but I couldn't justify taking my eyes off of the dry road ahead or taking my death-gripped hands from the steering wheel.

I maintained a good speed—slow enough not to let the water splash into my engine, causing a stall, but fast enough to make progress. It felt like I was moving in slow motion. The safety of the solid ground behind me was getting farther away. I felt so desperate to get to the other side that I wanted to climb out onto the hood of the car while it was moving so when I got close enough, I could just jump to get there quicker.

The flow of the water was strong, and the sound of it hitting the front, side, and bottom of my car was loud and troubling. Images of a part being torn from under the car occurred to me—not as a concern for damages to the car, but rather that it would result in a stall and permit the water to take me with it. I was surrounded by the force of the water, vibrating the car through the gas pedal, steering wheel, and seat.

As I looked ahead, I noticed I was driving in the middle of the road; the water's strong current from the right was pushing me to the left. However, no cars were coming from the other direction, so this didn't matter. I steered to the right to prevent the car from running off the road, but it wouldn't maneuver back to the right side of the road. I kept the steering wheel turned just enough to the right to maintain control. I wasn't worried about getting back to the right side; I was terrified that I wouldn't stay on the road at all. I imagined watching myself standing on the roof of my floating car from the perspective of a hovering news helicopter.

I knew my life was in jeopardy and thought I had as much of a chance of losing control of the car as I did of getting out safely. I wondered what it would have taken to make my tires lose traction for good. *What if the water gets one inch deeper? What if I drive one mile per hour faster or slower? Turn my steering wheel just a couple degrees more to the right? Or a small branch gets pushed into the side of the car?* I was waiting for the car to start floating and even felt that a few times the car may have momentarily lost contact with the asphalt, but I was determined to make it to the other side, so I kept my hands on the steering wheel and maintained my speed.

My heart was pounding like when I exercise and push my body to its absolute limit. But even this was different; the pounding was deep, like my heart was trying to push itself out of my chest. I was scared, but I continued to focus on getting through.

People had appeared ahead of me, standing outside of their parked cars and stopping cars from going into the water. They were now waving the cars in front of me to quickly get across, looking a bit agitated and somewhat panicked. I'm sure they thought we weren't too bright for trying to cross. I don't know if these were off-duty law enforcement or fire department employees, or just good citizens who knew when things were about to go bad, but they were right to think I was stupid for chancing it.

I was able to get back on the right side of the road as the water gradually became shallower and I approached the other side. When I'd made it across, I looked behind me at where I started. I was the last car to get through in both directions. The lady in the minivan that let me go in front of her had not tried to cross. A fire truck was trying to get to the water's edge to shut down that side of the road.

I knew I shouldn't have risked crossing the water and was very lucky I didn't get myself hurt or killed. It was deep enough and rushing fast enough that it probably should have swept me away. Finally in relative safety, I realized how tense I had been. The joints in my hands were aching and I let out a huge breath, relaxing for the first time since going into the water.

4:39 p.m. Once I got my bearings, I called Allison to tell her I'd made it through and was on my way home. She was glad, but didn't realize what I had just driven through or how scared I had been. I asked her if she'd been watching the news and if she knew whether or not there were any roads closed. She said they had mentioned that a lot of roads were closed but none that would affect my new route home. Before hanging up, she reminded me to be careful, just as she would any other day; however, this time there was just a hint of apprehension in her voice. "I'll see you in a little bit," she said, and we hung up.

4:45 p.m. I called my parents to tell them not to get on the roads. My mom told me about flooding in Columbia, Tennessee, where my brother lived, and that she thought they had water getting close to their house. I told her I'd give them a call once I got home safely.

4:47 p.m. I called my friend Steve Shaver, a sheriff's deputy that was on duty that day, and he gave me some back roads to take that he didn't think were flooded yet. Still, it took me more than an hour to make what should have been a twenty-five-minute trip. A little after five o'clock, I had finally arrived home.

4

Our Home

Our house was a small, ranch-style house that was built in the early 1980s. Three bedrooms were common among the houses in our neighborhood, but that is basically where the similarities ended. We were lucky enough to have a garage, while some around us had fireplaces or larger master bathrooms. Though we'd signed the papers a few days before, city records say that house officially became ours on May 1, 2008.

It was a good first house and it served us well for exactly two years to the day. The size was perfect for our little family. We loved the hardwood floors and the vaulted ceiling in the living room. I loved having a garage and a fenced-in backyard that our dogs could run around in. We worked hard to make it feel comfortable and look nice. I scraped the stucco from the ceilings and we painted every room in the house before we moved in. We wanted our first home to be perfect.

Our first child, Patrick, was born a year after we moved in. Allison spent a lot of time planning his nursery and created a room filled with the colors of the outdoors—sky blue, grass green, and sunny yellow. Joe, my artistic childhood friend and college roommate, came over and helped me paint clouds along the top of the walls all the way around the room. He spent an hour or two showing me how to do it using paintbrushes and sponges, and we included two clouds in the shape of a rocket and a plane that were hidden among the rest.

We had a mature Japanese maple tree right outside our kitchen window. In the spring of 2009, we watched a robin make her nest and lay three baby-blue eggs. For two weeks the robin worked diligently while she waited for them to hatch. Every day she would inspect and improve the nest by moving pieces of it around, sometimes leaving the nest and returning minutes later with another stick or string or piece of plastic, which she would place into the nest, no doubt in the exact spot it was needed.

Then one day I looked out and the chicks had hatched. It was beautiful to watch their reactions when they heard their mother approaching. Once, when the mother robin was away, I went outside with our camera to get a picture of the babies up close. When they heard me brushing up against the branches and leaves, they began chirping and squeaking and stuck their heads straight up into the air with their mouths wide open. Their necks were stretched up as far as they could go in an attempt to be the first one to get food.

Their skin was an almost translucent bright pink and their eyes were still sealed shut. Their feathers were thin and sporadic. As they stretched to greet their mom's beak, their heads wobbled because of their weak necks. Without getting too close, I snapped a few pictures just before the robin returned to feed her babies.

We watched these chicks grow. Their feathers grew longer and thicker and began the gradual shift to the black and burnt-red coloring that is characteristic of adult robins. And then one day they were gone and we could only hope they were safe.

In April of 2010, we watched again as a robin began making her nest close to the same spot. We were excited to watch the process again over the coming weeks.

We had done quite a bit of work outside and were anticipating a beautiful lawn as the spring of 2010 continued. We had a crape myrtle tree that we planted the summer before in honor of Patrick's birth, and we were looking forward to seeing its first bright red bloom. There was a guarantee on the tree that it would bloom its first year pending "an act of God." We also had just planted daylilies in our front flower bed. They were starting to sprout and would soon add some color to the yard.

5

The Approaching River

5:18 p.m. Not long after arriving home, I called my older brother, Adam, to see if things were okay in Columbia. He told me they were thinking about evacuating their home. The water had risen to their foundation and was surrounding the house. He'd watched the rising water in his backyard push his neighbor's toolshed into their swing set, sweeping both away. Allison and I offered them a place to stay if they needed it. Thankfully, the water around their house was a flash flood from a creek at the back of their property and receded before it could get inside their house.

We had a moderate level of anxiety, but with no reason to panic yet, we went on with our evening routine. We had an old threadbare blue rocking recliner that was now coated with a thin brown cover. Every time you rocked in it or moved in it in any way, it would squeak. As we relaxed for the evening, Allison sat in this chair playing "Where's Momma?" with one-year-old Patrick in her lap. She covered her face with a blue washcloth and Patrick immediately started smiling. She asked him where she was, and he looked at me with his beautiful smile. Chuckling, he looked back at her and tried to look around the washcloth to find her face. After several seconds he fell into her with a big, open-mouthed baby kiss on her washcloth-covered face. The washcloth fell off when he did this and he collapsed onto her chest and cuddled like there was no safer place on earth.

All that afternoon and evening, I watched as the water pooled at the bottom of our backyard. During periods of heavy rain, I monitored the yard, watching the clear rainwater trickle through the rich, green grass. The pooled water never came close to the house, but I would keep an eye out as the evening progressed.

A typical big storm will dump only a couple of inches of rain, and this system had already significantly exceeded that. With all the fuss from the news about potential flooding and seeing almost constant rain for so long, I watched as the rain got higher in my backyard than I had ever seen it. However, as the evening progressed, the water vanished. I relaxed since obviously the water was draining faster than it was coming in.

10:03 p.m. I got a call from my friend and neighbor Jonathan late that evening. He said the river was high and asked me to come across the street and help him move some of his stuff away from his shed that was on the low side of his property.

Jonathan and his wife Rebecca lived directly across the street from us. Jonathan frequently came over to our house to help me with projects and I often returned the favor. Whether it was lifting something heavy, borrowing tools, or helping to get a job done, we spent a lot of time with each other and had fun doing it. We are both teachers and always had something to talk about. Jonathan's belief in helping others would later save lives.

Jonathan and Rebecca's backyard gradually sloped down toward the river around ten feet in elevation. At the end of their property the land dramatically dropped another fifteen to twenty feet to the river. When I got there, the river was inches away from flowing over onto their yard. His toolshed was about fifteen feet away from the river and only about a foot higher than the water level.

When I saw the water as high as it was, I was surprised that I didn't hear the roar of a raging river. In fact, it was eerily quiet. The water was sneaking around the trees, giving a false sense of calm.

Jonathan said the local news wasn't expecting the water to crest for at least twenty-four hours; however, it looked pretty obvious to both of us that the water would reach his shed and wouldn't take too long to do so. We never expected the water to get high enough to reach his house.

Jonathan's next door neighbor, Kevin, was young and had arms that were built for moving heavy stuff. He could probably bench press a pickup truck off of me if I was stuck underneath it. So, naturally, we knocked on his door and asked for some help. He looked at us through sleepy eyes like we were crazy. Though he was impressed with how high the water was, he seemed to think it couldn't get much higher. He humored us anyway and helped us move Jonathan's important tools from the shed to the house as a light rain fell on us. We discussed the improbability of the water getting high enough to reach his house and I asked Jonathan to give me a call if it actually did. I was only half serious.

As we went to bed that night, the Harpeth River was starting to overflow its banks. While we slept in our dry, safe bed, people in parts of Middle Tennessee were fleeing the rising water. Nashville's flood had begun. Our flood would wait until morning.

Our first home on Beech Bend Drive before the flood. (Photo by Owen Grimenstein)

Allison and I taking a break from working on the house to pose for a picture. (Photo from Owen Grimenstein)

The newly hatched robins in our Japanese maple tree outside our kitchen window. (Photo by Owen Grimenstein)

Our house on April 13, 2010, about two weeks before the flood. The deck had not yet been completed.
(Photo courtesy of Google Earth)

Me standing on my newly finished deck just days before the flood. (Photo from Owen Grimenstein)

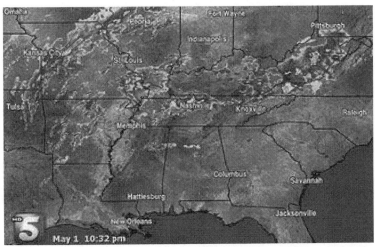

This is a radar shot from May 1, 2010, showing the second of the three major storm systems. (Photo courtesy of Channel 5 News)

This is a still shot from a video taken by Adam Grimenstein. A neighbor's floating shed knocked over a swing set just before both were swept away by rushing waters in Columbia, Tennessee, on May 1, 2010.

Allison and Patrick cuddling the night before evacuation. (Still shot from video by Owen Grimenstein)

II.

The Flood

". . . a small wall of water, about six inches maybe, just began to wash right on in to the chapel from the back pew all the way up to the altar. In retrospect it seems like it was in slow motion, but you could actually hear it. And I saw parishioners, beginning at the back but also moving forward, jump off their knees because they had been on their knees to pray during this prayer."

—Reverend Leigh Spruill tells of his experience during a church service at St. George's Episcopal Church to the 2010 Digital History Project through the Nashville Public Library.

6

Evacuation

Sunday, May 2, 2010

4:40 a.m. Allison and I woke to the sound of a ringing phone. Even in my post-deep-sleep confusion, my first thought was of the river. I picked up my cell phone and read Jonathan's name on the glowing display screen. "Hey, what's going on?" I thought he was going to tell me that his shed was surrounded by water and he needed me to help him salvage it. Instead he said, "The river is up to our back porch and we are leaving. I think it's about time you two discussed if you are going to leave or stay."

I later heard the story of how his wonderful dog, Luke, woke them up with his barking. Luke often barked when he knew a squirrel or rabbit was outside, but this bark was different. This was not an excited bark but a warning. When they let him outside to do his business, Luke splashed through the river that had now reached their back porch. They saw how high the water was and Rebecca immediately started packing. Jonathan called me and every other neighbor he had a phone number for. He also went house to house banging on doors and bedroom windows alerting several immediate neighbors. Many of the people living around us credit him for getting them out in time.

I got out of bed and looked outside. I could see Jonathan running around packing their car and splashing through water in their front yard. Everywhere behind his house was covered in water. I couldn't believe how much water there had to be to make it that high. And although I sensed the significance of what I was seeing, I did not feel the urgency. I was impressed but still felt that it would be impossible for the water to get in our house.

I told Allison what was happening and laid back down. We briefly discussed what we were going to do and decided to let Patrick sleep some more before making a decision, thinking we had a couple of hours before the water would get too close to us. However, since there is no noticeable difference in the elevation between Jonathan's house and our house, in hindsight, it was not our wisest decision.

We laid in bed until shortly before 5:20 a.m. I tossed and turned while my mind played out many different scenarios, all of which included the safety of my family being in jeopardy. So, I got out of bed and looked out the window again. In those forty minutes, the water had reached the road and was covering the majority of Jonathan's front yard. I immediately told Allison, "We should go ahead and get ready to leave." I kept a calm but urgent attitude so as not to panic her.

5:20 a.m. Allison called her mom to let her parents know what was going on. She woke up and fed Patrick and started to get him ready to leave. I started packing a change of clothes, toiletries, enough to get me through one night of being away.

5:26 a.m. I called my parents to tell them we were evacuating, my voice nervous and unsteady. My mom told me to slow down so she could understand me. The conversation didn't last long, but it was enough to get her worried.

Around this time Allison finished getting Patrick ready and she helped me pack. She grabbed our external hard drive, which carried all of our pictures that we had taken the last few years, our wedding album, files from our filing cabinet, and a lock box that held our passports, social security cards, birth certificates, and other valuable documents. Allison saw the Bible that I received when I was baptized and grabbed it, throwing it along with some other stuff into a box. She packed a change of clothes for herself, assuming, as I did, we would be back the next day.

Just in case the water did get high, we put a couple of things on the bed and some other important stuff, including our electrical wires and surge protectors, up high on bookshelves, desks, and tables. Worst-case scenario, I imagined the carpet getting a little wet.

The rain was light and intermittent. I noticed with each trip to our cars that the water in the front yard was getting steadily deeper. I used the back door, going around the house each time, because the flooding in the backyard wasn't close enough to the house to have to walk through water yet. I didn't want to step through water and then track it in the house and get the floors wet. This took longer but my feet wouldn't get as wet as they would if I went through the front door. Every time I did come back in the house, I made sure to wipe my feet on the mat, knowing that since we were going to be leaving the house, any water on the floor would not be cleaned up for a while.

On one of my trips out to the car, I saw Jonathan putting his kayak on his front porch before hurrying off to do something else. He would later tell me that he knew the shed was going to be lost, along with the kayak, which was attached to it. He had waded out to the shed and brought the kayak to the front porch so it wouldn't get swept away. Because of the improbability of how high the water would get and because he was running out of time, he didn't tie the kayak down.

As the water got deeper and closer to our house, I became more anxious for us to get out and more aware that the water might get high enough to reach the floors after all. I began taking the shorter route to the car through the front door. During my last few trips, the water was starting to cover the wheels on the car and I was running through ankle- and shin-deep water. I also stopped wiping my feet when coming back inside, accepting my squeaking shoes against the hardwood floors as a necessity to saving these last few things and getting away safely.

Allison knew it was important to hurry and noticed that my pace was getting quicker each time I came back inside the house, but being busy packing and watching Patrick, she hadn't looked outside in a while. Finally, after returning from a trip to the car and realizing that time was getting very short for us to get out safely, I said, "We have to leave *now*."

When we walked outside, it was still raining. I had just turned off the circuit breaker and locked the doors as Allison began to panic. This was the first time she had seen how high the water had gotten since watching Jonathan and Rebecca packing their car after he first called us. Shaking and crying, she began saying, "We are never going to get out of here" over and over. She thought that Jonathan and Rebecca got out and that we were going to be stuck. I told her, loudly, "We will be able to if we leave now."

Our two small dogs were outside with us but one wouldn't walk through the water, and Allison and I kept yelling at her to get in the car. We had our hands full with Patrick, our other dog, and half-empty boxes that we didn't have time to fill up. The stress of the situation also increased the intensity of how Allison and I were speaking to each other. We remember that we were arguing, though we don't know what about, because afterward we were embarrassed that our next-door neighbors Dave and Catherine, who were outside evaluating whether or not to leave, could hear us.

Our adrenaline and emotions were running high, but Patrick was so interested in what was going on that he just looked around at the water and stared at us. Thankfully, he didn't feel the danger. He only knew the limitless safety of being in his parents' arms.

Shortly after 6:00 a.m. By the time we left, less than an hour and a half after the call from Jonathan, the water was coming from both the front and back of the house. It had risen to the foundation in the front and was touching the bottom step of the deck in the back. The water was halfway up the tires on the cars and was unlike the muddy water I had driven through the day before. Seeing the bright green grass through the clear water showed me that it didn't belong there. The clean standing water that was around the house was level with the river but had yet to become tainted by the dirty river water.

Allison took one car with both dogs and I took the other with Patrick. The road to the right of our driveway appeared to have more standing water on it. To the left, there was very little to no water in sight. Jonathan had moved his truck a house or two down the road in that direction because it was slightly higher and drier than his driveway, in hopes it would not flood. Neither direction had any low areas to drive through that I could think of, and going left would be close to the same distance, so I told Allison to go left.

Two separate neighbors who left before we did, took the direction I told Allison to go because they, too, must have thought it looked less dangerous. Jonathan and Rebecca had fled in that direction. However, they quickly came upon water that looked too dangerous to cross. Jonathan told me later that, with his wife and little girl at risk, he switched to survival mode and drove through a lady's yard to get around the water. The owner was right there outside when he did this and started yelling something at him with her hands in the air. Her body language said, "What do you think you are doing?"

Two doors down from Jonathan, our neighbors Matt and Tessa's van stalled with their children inside as they attempted to escape, possibly in the same area where Jonathan and Rebecca had to drive through the lady's yard. Luckily they were able to wade to another house, where someone they knew was leaving and got them out safely.

Dave and Catherine, who had decided to leave shortly after us, also took this direction. They left after us, and after driving through so much water, they temporarily lost their brakes. When they circled around the neighborhood and got to the end of Beech Bend Drive, they rolled down the hill with no brakes and through the intersection at Old Harding Pike. Fortunately for them it was early enough in the morning that the traffic lights were still flashing and no other cars were around, which could have been disastrous had it been any later in the day.

Had we gone left out of our driveway, as I had initially told Allison to do, we probably would have gotten in a situation

45

similar to the ones I just described. I'm not sure what our options would have been had that happened, but it's a pretty good guess that this story would have turned out differently. Thankfully, Allison didn't hear me, or forgot, and took a right. At the time I was upset with her for going the way common sense should have told her not to go. Later on, after hearing these stories from our neighbors, I was relieved.

On our street, right in front of our house, the water was up to our bumpers as we slowly drove through two flooded spots in the road that were easily twenty to forty yards long each. With the baby in the car I was worried, of course, that the car would stall and I would have to carry him through the water back to the house and be stranded. At this point, the water wasn't noticeably moving, so I wasn't worried about getting washed away with him. Luckily, we made it through and were able to get on the higher road safely. We would have to drive east on Interstate 40 as westbound was already shut down at the next exit down from ours and all other interstates in the area were shut down in multiple places due to high water. Allison's brother and his family lived in Mt. Juliet, so that is where we decided to go.

I did not stop for anything. The only thought in my mind was getting my family out of harm's way. I wasn't thinking about anyone else and I'm ashamed that, at the time, I did not consider helping others. I was in survival mode and running on autopilot at that point. Patrick was in the back seat and I knew we were possibly seconds away from getting stranded and possibly minutes away from getting swept away.

However, when Jonathan and Rebecca were escaping the neighborhood, he noticed a house with no lights on, so he assumed no one had woken up the lady who lived there. He stopped the car and banged on the door until she did wake up. Even in a time of potential peril, he wasn't thinking only of himself and his family. His dedication to serving others remained strong. To this day, the lady still claims that Jonathan saved her life.

6:06 a.m. Allison called her sister-in-law Carrie as soon as we got on Interstate 40 and told her we were heading their way. The exit where she was calling from, exit 196, would be under water later that day. Our adrenaline was pumping so hard that we were speeding through the hard rain, hitting standing water and hydroplaning. I couldn't help it; I knew to slow down, especially with Patrick in the car, but something wouldn't let me do it. I kept telling myself to make my foot lighten the pressure on the accelerator but my foot wouldn't listen. I was having a hard time coming down from flight mode.

As soon as we got in east Nashville the rain stopped so suddenly it became weirdly quiet; the only audible noise was the screeching of my windshield wipers across the drying windshield. The road was actually so dry I wondered if they had received any rain at all in the last twenty-four hours. Even though we were out of any immediate danger and had no real reason to be driving fast anymore, we continued to speed down the interstate.

Everything outside my car went by in a blur as I thought about the distant and unrealistic possibilities of what was coming next, what I should have grabbed, and how I could have been more efficient getting us ready. I had no idea that what we had just left behind would later be referred to by US representative Jim Cooper as ground zero for this natural disaster.[17]

7

Watching and Waiting

6:42 a.m. We arrived in Mt. Juliet, and Allison called her mom to tell her we were safe. Carrie, Allison's sister-in-law, was waiting at the door for us. By the time Allison got out of the car, Carrie was out in the front yard. They embraced and cried together. I unpacked what I could in one or two trips and then went to watch the news with Allison and her family.

The local Channel 4 News was turned on in the living room and they were broadcasting news of the flood. One of the stories was about Interstate 40 eastbound, the way we had just come, which had just been shut down due to flooding in at least one place. We had missed it by mere minutes. Some of the water that we had driven through was not just standing water, but was the river beginning to overtake the road.

Now that my family was safe, I wanted to go back home—not only to try to save more belongings but also to see what was going on. However, seeing how high the water had gotten, I knew I wouldn't be able to make it back even if I tried. Jonathan also had the same thought, telling me later that he tried to go back to his house just thirty minutes after they left. By the time he got there, the roads into the neighborhood were completely impassable and he watched as a woman walked through the water holding only her small child and her purse.

We watched the news all day. We watched as a portable building from a nearby school floated in the rushing waters down Interstate 24 and disintegrated when it crashed into abandoned cars. We watched video after video of rescues and destruction. There were updates on people who were missing or confirmed dead, business and school closings, and repeated firsthand accounts from eyewitnesses and victims. We couldn't keep our eyes off of the television.

12:43 p.m. I received this phone message from the school system I worked for:

> *"Hello parents and staff. This is Carol Birdsong, Communications Director for Williamson County Schools. Please listen to this entire message. Superintendent Dr. Mike Looney, has been working with emergency management personnel across the county today. Because of the hazardous flooding conditions throughout the county and based on emergency management's recommendation, we will not have school in Williamson County tomorrow, Monday, May 3."*

The waters in my brother's backyard were rising again. At the exact time that I received the call announcing schools would be closed, Adam was videotaping his backyard again, and on camera he said, "Right now we are concerned about Owen and Allison, because their subdivision has been on the news about the flooding. So, we are worried about their house." Luckily, the water around his house didn't get higher than it had the day before and they were spared once more by just a few inches.

News Channel 4 had a camera on our road and throughout the day would periodically show updates. We watched as the waters rose. As the day progressed, the water slowly consumed a red car that was parked on the street not far from the camera and crew. I kept expecting to see the owner come and get it before it was too late but he or she never did. Each time the news switched over for an update, another portion of the car was farther under water, until it had disappeared completely. The river had swallowed the car, no longer considering it an obstacle to move around. In fact, the surface of the water moved over the car freely and smoothly like it had never been there to begin with.

The news reporter who was stationed at that spot on Beech Bend Drive said they had watched someone get rescued who had been clinging to a tree near where the reporters were standing. They showed close-ups of some of the houses, which were also going deeper and deeper under water. We watched as the water overtook the base of their front doors and windows and eventually covered the doorknobs and above. Our house was far enough away from the camera that we couldn't see it, but we could imagine what our house was starting to look like.

Even though our house wasn't on higher elevation compared to the houses we were seeing on television, I remained optimistic that somehow, miraculously, our house was different and wouldn't be significantly flooded. For many hours Allison and I watched the news with her brother and sister-in-law, and I continued to have these irrationally confident thoughts.

I was optimistic until I saw the man whose backyard bordered our yard get rescued on a boat along with his wife and two dogs. I initially hoped that maybe their house was fine and they just couldn't get out because the roads were blocked by water. However, when the news interviewed the wife, she said she had been waiting on their roof for help. Knowing their house's elevation was no different than ours, I gave up hope that our home would have minimal damage. I became quiet and disheartened. As my optimism tapered off, so did the rain, finally ending around 8:30 Sunday night.

Allison had been talking all day about all the things we weren't able to save from the house, such as her wedding dress, photos, and the bowl I used when I proposed to her. We were all desperate to get to the house to try and salvage these treasured items. Allison's brother, Drew, felt helpless because we could only sit around his home while the contents of our home were soaking in muddy water. He wanted to help somehow and couldn't just sit and watch TV.

At some point late Sunday afternoon, Drew disappeared from the house. No one knew where he had gone. When he returned home and Carrie inquired about where he had been, Drew announced to me and Allison, "Well, one way or another, we are getting in your house tomorrow."

Allison, Carrie, and I looked at one another with puzzled expressions. As we all wondered the same thing, Carrie was the first to ask, "What did you do?"

He replied with a nonchalant shrug, "I bought a raft."

8

A Raft

Monday, May 3, 2010. Drew and I drove out to Bellevue on a
beautiful Monday morning. Most of the roads were already
dry, and any moisture remaining could just as well have been
the leftover morning dew from the cool night. Driving through
neighborhoods that did not flood did not help with the surreal
feeling I was experiencing. Except for the anxiety of
wondering what I was going to find, it felt like a normal day.
It certainly didn't seem as if we could be driving toward a
natural disaster area.

As we approached Beech Bend, everything, at first, looked
normal. I thought maybe the news had been filming the wrong
place, or this all had been just an elaborate and highly
inappropriate prank where I would get to my house and
hundreds of people would be waiting there to yell, "Surprise!
We got you!" At the time, I knew these thoughts were not
logical, but they seemed more realistic than what was actually
happening.

We got our first glimpse of the flood while sitting at the light
on the corner of Beech Bend and Old Harding Pike. There
were several police cars blocking Old Harding Pike past the
light. On the other side of the parked cruisers, the Harpeth
River was drowning a golf driving range in more than fifteen
feet of water. The trailer that the business used had washed

away, and the water was just inches from touching the traffic lights on the road in front of the golf center.

Drew and I proceeded up the already-dry first half of Beech Bend. But as we went down a small hill, we saw the water's edge. The street went from normal, middle-class, ranch-style homes to a natural disaster area within one home on each side of the street. One house had no damage while their neighbor had lost almost everything. It immediately became apparent that the news hadn't been lying, this wasn't a hoax, and I wasn't dreaming after all. Yet I maintained the belief that my house might still be okay.

We drove up to the spot on Beech Bend where the Channel 4 cameras had been the previous day. The water had clearly gone down several feet, as we could now see about half of the red car that was parked on the road. There were many cars parked along the portion of the road that had not flooded, and these belonged to people looking at the devastation for themselves. Drew had two life jackets, one adult and one child. He put on the adult life jacket and I attached the child's life jacket to the back side of my belt. We took turns pumping up the raft with a manual hand pump, put our phones, keys, and wallets into Ziploc bags, and walked toward the water. The water appeared to be two to three feet deep and had a brisk current in several places.

A police officer was waiting on the road at the water's edge with his arms crossed and asked where we were going. I told him my house was not far from here. He replied, "You guys can't go in there. People are missing and have died from getting in there already." He hesitated after saying this, then continued, "Plus, the mayor just told us to not let anyone go in." He pointed to the sky at one of the helicopters that was circling the neighborhood and said, "That's him up there." I didn't have the emotional energy to argue or plead and just stood there staring at him in exhaustion and disbelief. He looked at me. I don't think he had the heart to follow through with keeping us out of the water, or figured we'd find a way to get in regardless, so he said, "If you want to go, you'll need to find another way." In my mind I took this to mean, "Find somewhere where I can't see you."

Drew and I walked away carrying the raft and soon were cutting through yards and hopping a few chain link fences before finally ending up on a neighboring street, Footpath Terrace, in shin- to knee-deep waters. It was obvious that the water was shallower on this road and didn't have as much current as Beech Bend, so we deemed it much safer. I knew where I was and how to get to my house from this location, so we decided to continue the way we were going. We chose to pull the raft behind us as neither of us was very experienced with rafting, and if we had tried to get in the raft, we would have scraped along the road in a few places where the water was shallow.

For the most part, the water had only a slight current, which gave us a workout as we walked through it. In several places, however, it would get about knee-deep or higher, moving at intimidating speeds. We were able to move laterally to find places like fire hydrants, fences, telephone poles, cars, and so forth that broke up the current enough for us to get through. Taking it one slow step at a time, we made sure we had secure footing before taking the next step.

It was a long, wet walk once we turned onto Harpeth Bend Drive. We felt like we were walking through a ghost town in the Wild West, except instead of dirt and tumbleweeds, water flowed around and through these houses. Every single house that we passed had been abandoned and sat empty. We talked very little as we looked at the noticeable water lines on the exteriors of the houses, amazed at how high the water had risen. Windows were broken from debris that had been forced into them with tremendous power. Mailboxes were missing, and around us was debris from collapsed structures. I had plenty of time to imagine what my house would look like.

I looked up at the beautiful blue sky. The few clouds that were present were fluffy and white. The birds sang their songs. I desperately wanted to look down and see the water gone, all part of a bad dream. It was strange to see the juxtaposition between the extremes of nature. Above me was beauty and peace; below was destruction and heartache. Staring ahead and seeing both at the same time felt like a superimposed picture that only trick photography could achieve. This picture, however, I could not dismiss as having been manipulated. It was reality.

We passed cars that had been completely engulfed with the floodwater, leaving the interior of the cars coated in mud. Upholstered fabric was falling apart and dangling from the ceilings of some as though they had been sitting in a junkyard for years. Several cars had been abandoned by their owners in the middle of the street after stalling in the waters as they tried to escape.

It took about thirty minutes for us to walk the equivalent of three-tenths of a mile before finally arriving at the house directly behind mine, the house belonging to the couple that we saw get rescued from the roof. We could see a current, but since it was going toward my house, we didn't have to worry about paddling and could concentrate more on steering. The problem was that both backyards have a negative slope from the house until they meet in the middle, forming a "V" shape, meaning it was going to be deep.

About 10:13 a.m. We climbed into the raft and started paddling. We used the neighbor's aluminum fence as a guide as long as we could in order to shorten the distance that we would have to be at the mercy of the water. It quickly disappeared beneath us and my house, rising from the water, came clearly into view. The current, which was coming from our backs, allowed us an easier time getting to the house.

10:16 a.m. Since the water was level with the floor of the house and with the deck, when we got close enough, we were able to slide onto the deck like a boat onto a beach.

The first thing we noticed was that the water had slammed the deck into the back of the house. The railings were pushed through the wall into the house on the right side, and broke some of the glass on the bay window of Patrick's room on the left. As I crossed the deck to the back door, it felt slightly buoyant and unstable under my feet. Later I would see that the water had pulled the deck beams out of the ground, along with the concrete that was anchoring it. All I could think of was all of the work I had put into rebuilding the deck over the past couple of weeks.

I noticed the Japanese maple still in its original location next to the deck; it was discolored more than halfway up from the dirt left behind by the water. The water had gotten high enough to cover the new robin's nest, which left me wondering what would happen next for the robin—whether she would have to start over somewhere else or be able to use the nest as-is.

Although I tried to look through the back deck windows while I was getting my keys out, I couldn't see anything because of the dirty film that was covering the glass. The windows were also steamed up from the humidity inside the house. I struggled to get the key in the keyhole because dirt was lodged inside the dead bolt.

I pictured everything wet and dirty. I figured, in my still unrelenting mixture of ignorance and optimism, we could wipe all the furniture down, replace some drywall, and then go on living our lives. I even assumed the floors would be fine after drying them out a little bit.

As I prepared to open the door, I closed my eyes and prayed. I didn't know what to pray for or what I should even say. It was a prayer of only two words: *Please God*. I paused to leave the rest to empty space.

Opening the door, I stepped inside and immediately felt whatever optimism that remained in me drain away. The unrealistic hope I had held on to disappeared. Disbelief and shock took over as I looked around my house.

It was darker inside than it would have normally been on a sunny day, and it appeared as if all the windows were covered with curtains, when in reality it was the muddy residue on the glass that prohibited the sunlight from shining through. Any bright colors were now dulled and blended in with everything else.

Without any power, the house was humid, the air still and thick. The smell of stale, musty water reminded me of my childhood and the way my clothes smelled after running around the neighborhood all day, playing tackle football in the mud or running through the woods.

The furniture was in disarray and had become a jumbled, overturned heap of debris. The water had gotten about five and a half feet high inside the house, lifting tall, heavy items that floated and had fallen over when the waters receded. Just about everything ended up on its side and in another part of the room, or even in another part of the house. There were DVDs in our master bathroom that had floated from the bedroom at the opposite end of the house. My neighbor Rebecca later told me she imagined the furniture in our houses floating slowly and calmly, moving like toys in a draining bathtub.

My mind couldn't fully grasp the reality of where I was and what was going on. I went back and forth between thinking that I was in someone else's house and then remembering I was in my home, which elicited feelings of angst and hurt.

The floors were still gleaming with moisture. Anywhere we stepped or anywhere something was moved we could see the sharp contrast between the floor with and without the mud. On the hardwood my shoes squeaked and slipped, but on the carpet my steps squished and splashed.

Our nice china cabinet had floated and turned on its back. Somehow, all of the stemware from our wedding had stayed upright, so when the cabinet came to rest on the floor, on its back, the stemware was sitting upright on the back wall of the cabinet instead of on their sides. Not a single china plate or wine glass was damaged, but all were full of cloudy water, as though they were ready to toast the river for a job well done.

The furniture had floated, causing just about everything that we had put up high to fall into the water. When the bed had floated and tilted, most of the items that we had put on top of it became unbalanced and fell off or just absorbed the water after the sheets and comforter became soaked. Trash from trash cans was spread around the house.

The fridge had floated and opened, causing food to spread throughout the house. When the water receded, the fridge came to rest partially on the kitchen counter, not even touching the ground. The kitchen counters, where we prepared our food, were muddy and dripping. Cabinets and drawers had opened, and some of the contents were flushed out of them.

The baby bottle drying rack had fallen apart, some of it knocked on its side on the counter and the rest on the floor. That drying rack, which once was the cleanest part of our entire house, was now dripping and holding muddy water. This stayed with me as a symbol of how something can drastically transition from being a perfect representation of cleanliness to a dirty piece of plastic that you would find in a dump.

Almost everything was coated in a layer of brown mud, including Patrick's bright green fitted crib sheet. Our light-colored carpet was now a dark brown. The walls were noticeably dirty and some of the drywall had bubbled up. There were two or three horizontal lines of dirt on the walls, indicating where the water got to its highest point and where the water must have sat stagnant for a while.

The comfortable rocking chair that we used so often had floated to the other side of Patrick's room. We read to Patrick and rocked him to sleep in that chair. We would swivel in it and look out his bay window at our backyard as he slept in our arms or just cuddled. This special spot in our home was now dripping dirty water, and those precious moments we had were quickly becoming distant memories.

Floodwaters are known for being filthy. Chemicals and sewage mix with the water . . . and animals die. In the days following the flood, we saw posters of missing pets. I heard one story of an elderly woman who got stranded outside with her dog. As the waters rose, she had to climb a tree and make the devastating decision to let her dog go.

With the filthiness of the floodwater forefront in our minds, we adhered to the FEMA authorities' recommendation to get rid of any porous furniture regardless of whether it might be salvageable. For this reason, we would end up throwing away a lot of stuff even though we possibly could have saved it. We didn't want to risk it, especially with a baby in the house putting his mouth on everything.

Drew and I did not want to spend too much time in the house, and we had limited space to put things in the raft. We looked around for a minute or two while Drew took pictures with his phone. We searched for a few things on Allison's list of must-haves and things we wanted to save if possible. I grabbed mud-soaked photo albums, including a scrapbook of my childhood that my mom had worked on for years and had recently given me. We got Allison's wedding dress, which was now brown, and a box of her childhood keepsakes. Although these precious items had gotten wet, we hoped we could at least clean off some of it before it did too much damage. If we cleaned it quickly enough, perhaps it wouldn't dry and allow stains to set in. A dry-cleaner was able to restore the wedding dress to its original form in a process that took several months. Nearly all of the pictures were too damaged to salvage. We had almost retrieved everything we wanted to get but, before we could do that, there was one more item that we had to find.

9

A Bowl

I was not looking for a serious relationship when I first met Allison. Because of the negative experience I had with a prior relationship, I was determined not to lead this girl on. At first, when we went on dates, I would make her pay for her own meal so she couldn't possibly be confused with what my expectations were for the relationship. She still likes to give me a hard time about this, of course, and brings it up to embarrass me in social gatherings.

This plan didn't last long, however. I was soon head over heels for her and shifted my focus to not letting her get away. We made our relationship exclusive and worked hard on maintaining a successful long-distance relationship until we both graduated from college and she moved to Nashville to be near me.

When she shifted from someone I didn't want to lose to someone I absolutely couldn't spend the rest of my life without, I bought her a ring. Before I could give her the ring, however, I had to come up with a plan on how to propose.

So in December of 2004, I went to one of those paint-your-own-pottery places and painted two almost identical bowls. At the bottom of one of the bowls I painted, "Will you marry me?" I wrapped the bowl without the words and left it in her apartment. The next day, I told her I got her something. She opened the bowl while I was at work and over the phone told me she loved it.

After work, I went over to her apartment and surprised her with her favorite ice cream. She had fallen asleep on the couch waiting for me. At the time, I was working at Blockbuster (my kids will now have to go look up what that store was), so I did not get off work until late. I woke her up and went to the kitchen to serve ice cream, switching the bowls. While she ate I stayed calm, not giving away my anticipation, while we had trivial discussions about how our days went and other unmemorable topics.

As she was finishing her ice cream, she saw some writing peeking through on the bottom of the bowl. She scraped through the remaining ice cream with her spoon, confused as to how she could have missed seeing words there before. By the time she realized what it said, I was down on one knee, proposing. We were married the following July.

10

The Return Trip

Inside the house, Drew was on a mission. Knowing how much the proposal bowl meant to Allison, Drew searched the house until he finally found it sitting on top of a console table that was near its original position by the front door. Amazingly, the console table had floated upright several feet before landing safely back on its narrow legs without dumping anything that was sitting on top of it. Along with the bowl, other items that didn't get wet were two library books and a Netflix movie that were waiting to be returned. Drew put the bowl in the almost-full raft, satisfied that he could give Allison some level of solace.

Before we left I called Jonathan, telling him that our houses were still standing and offering a brief summary of what it looked like in my house. I updated him on how high the water was on the streets so he had a basic idea on how long he had before they could try to get out to their house. I also noticed his kayak sitting awkwardly on his front porch like it had just floated up and come back down to rest halfway on the porch railing. The kayak, which is designed to float and glide through water, stayed where it was, yet a large outdoor trash can from somewhere else in the neighborhood had traveled to their front porch and rested against it.

There was also a pretty large structure in their front yard wedged in between two trees. I couldn't place what it was, but I mentioned it to him and asked if there was anything that he needed me to get out of the house. He told me there was nothing that was worth risking my life for, and we hung up.

We couldn't go down Beech Bend because the water was still deep and moving too rapidly for our comfort level and safety, making our best option to leave the way we'd come in, even though the waters were deep and moving in the opposite direction of the way we wanted to go. It would also give us a little more room for error if we lost control. We couldn't really get in the raft as there wasn't any room left; plus, we were worried about the weight.

We each swam with one arm holding on to the raft, which was aimed for the closest above-water part of the neighbor's fence. This would be the shortest distance we could travel without having anything to stop us from being swept away. We had to swim hard, fighting the current, aiming to the right of the fence so that the current would pull us to the left. We really didn't want to overshoot the fence. The water was very deep in between the houses, somewhere between ten to fifteen feet. I am sure we swam over our crape myrtle tree that had been planted the year before.

Drew was in front and, eventually, found the fence with his feet. He was able to get shallow enough on the fence that he could grab it with one hand, guiding me to it until I found it with my feet. The current was pretty strong, and just as I found the fence with my foot, he lost his grip on the fence and the water started pulling him away from it. I couldn't see him, but I could see that the raft was twisting away from the fence. Thankfully, I was able to hold on to the fence with my feet until he gained control and was able to swim back to the fence.

Once we were both on the fence, we used it to guide us back to shallower water.

We could hear a cat's cry coming from the house next to the neighbor's house, whose fence we were using as a life line. I looked up and saw it stuck on the roof. I imagined how it got there, wondering how long it had to swim before finding a way to get up there or whether it ever even got wet from anything but the rain. I wanted to help, but we were exhausted and didn't have access to a ladder. We had to leave it and hope it would be rescued or able to get down on its own when the water receded.

Our wet clothes clung to our skin as we left the house behind us. Exhausted and mostly in silence, we traveled back the way we came. The water had already receded a couple of inches from when we first arrived, but the walk seemed longer than before, since I now had time to dwell on what I had just seen. Our home and cherished possessions had been turned into nothing but a muddy pile that was worth nothing, monetarily or emotionally.

11:45 a.m. Since we couldn't carry the raft and everything in it over several fences, we had to "dock" on the dry road where we initially tried to get in the water. As we got out of the raft, a police officer (different from the one we spoke with earlier) casually walked over to us. I thought we were going to get a ticket; however, the officer only asked me where I lived and for my identification—he wanted to make sure the items on the raft were mine. Without reprimand or further chitchat, he left us and walked back to the squad car to talk with the first officer.

I sat down on the edge of the raft and waited for Drew to get his car so we could load it. There was a small crowd of onlookers nearby talking and taking pictures of the water and flooded houses, and I could tell a couple of people wanted to come talk to me. I sat there wondering if they were just rubbernecking tourists gawking at someone else's anguish or other victims of humanity's failed attempt to control Mother Nature.

I was exhausted. I wanted privacy. Most of these people tried not to make eye contact, but one woman and, presumably her daughter, walked up to me and asked, "What's it like back there?" She told me where they lived and asked if I had been that far back. We had, but I wasn't sure which house was theirs exactly. And yet, it didn't matter; they were all the same. I told her how high the water line was on all of the houses around there. That is all I could tell her. Their reaction was subdued. Maybe they had already heard the same thing and were expecting it, but hoping someone else would have better news.

We loaded Drew's SUV and began the long drive home. I was full of mixed emotions as I stared out the side window in a semi-trance, thinking of what we had lost, the reality of what had happened really hitting me for the first time. I thought about the houses that we were passing and how they hadn't lost a thing and how lucky they were.

We passed one house in my neighborhood where the homeowner was cutting his front yard. For a moment, I couldn't believe that he had the audacity to cut his grass. Didn't he know what was going on? People were going through a devastating ordeal and he was using a push mower on his front lawn! I thought this was insensitive to those of us who had lost so much, including our lawn mowers, and he should have thought about that. What I was going through

66

made me quite egocentric at the time, and I felt as though everyone else should be as appalled and hurt as I was. Later, I understood that what he was doing should have been no more offensive than someone else going out to eat somewhere. I may have even done the same thing had my house been spared and my grass needed to be cut. After all, the river was still up and he couldn't do a lot to help. For all I knew, he could have been planning to commit hours to volunteering in the coming days.

I also thought about all of the hard work we had put into making our house a home. It felt as though it had all been a waste of time, effort, and money. I started to think about all of the individual things that I lost. For years after the flood, Allison and I would be reminded of something and think, *I wonder where that is?* and quickly remember, *Oh, yeah. I guess that was lost too.* During this trip home, I almost cried a couple of times, but didn't want to lose it yet. I just wanted to be with Allison.

When we got to Drew and Carrie's house, I wasn't ready to go inside yet, so I took my time grabbing a few things from the car. As I stood shaking behind the SUV, I put my head down to my chest, closed my eyes, and said, "Please God, help us." I wasn't ready to face Allison yet. I wasn't strong enough for myself and knew I couldn't be the strength she needed. I told myself that it was okay for us to be weak together and went inside.

I walked into the house to find Allison sitting on the floor, sobbing. Drew had shown her and Carrie the pictures he took on his phone, and she broke down when she saw Patrick's room. I did my best to comfort her. Seeing how upset she was, Drew went to the kitchen to clean the proposal bowl he had retrieved and handed it to her hoping it would make her feel better. She cried even harder at seeing this bowl. We embraced and sat on the floor in their kitchen as she sobbed. Although I felt like crying, it still wasn't the right time. I wasn't ready to give in and acknowledge that we had lost almost everything.

By the time we returned from our trip to the house, people had already begun to donate boxes of toys and clothes for Patrick. Carrie had sent out requests to her friends, and people can't resist helping a baby. The rest of the afternoon and evening was spent cleaning pictures and documents, dropping off the wedding dress at a dry cleaners, and watching the news. Carrie and our niece, Samantha, set to work on the recovered photo albums, doing their best to salvage our memories.

In the end, our trip out to the house didn't save much, especially considering the high risk. Waiting until the next day may have had the same results. Drew commented to me later that perhaps we did it in order to have some modicum of control in an uncontrollable situation. We could go back to the house and save some of our stuff and the flood wasn't going to stop us. We couldn't sit around and do nothing. We needed to take some kind of action, to fight back the only way we knew how.

That afternoon, while trying to process the day's events, I received another call from the school district. This time it stated that schools would be open, although the superintendent later would give people who were directly affected by the flood "Natural Disaster days" so that teachers and staff could miss work without having to use sick or personal days. Students who couldn't attend school also received leeway. That lasted the rest of the week:

"Hello parents and staff. This is Carol Birdsong. Please listen to this entire message. School will be open in Williamson County tomorrow, Tuesday, May 4, but we will open two hours late . . . There are still some roads across the county that are closed, so bus drivers will be using discretion based on reported road conditions. All employees should report at the regular time . . ."

Jonathan and Rebecca found some family members in Bellevue who hadn't been flooded and were staying with them. Jonathan called that night around 8:45 and said that he had been told the water was down low enough that we could drive straight up to our houses, though he had not been there yet. Since I had already been out there and got some of the things we considered to be most important, and since nighttime would prohibit us from getting much done, I told him we would wait until morning to return.

You can see how the Harpeth River surrounds Beech Bend Drive and Harpeth Bend. The water came from both sides of the neighborhood. (Photo courtesy Google Earth)

Man looks in a flooded vehicle. (Photo by Erik England, courtesy of *Nashville Scene*).

Our neighborhood on Monday morning while the water was still three feet high, or about level with our floorboards inside the house. Drew and I were in the house at the time this picture was taken. (Photo courtesy of Sam Swift)

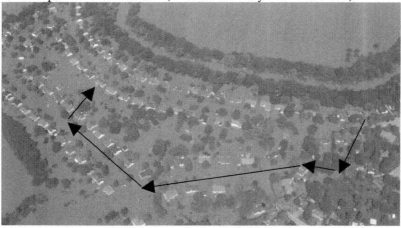

This is the route we took to get to the house. We cut through a few yards before we got onto Footpath Terrace and then turned right onto Harpeth Bend. (Photo courtesy of Sam Swift)

This picture was taken Monday morning while we were in the house. The raft is still parked on the back porch. (Photo courtesy of Sam Swift)

The black line marks the flow of the river. The path we took to get to the house is in white. We used the neighbor's fence at the top of his backyard, then tried to take a straight line to the back porch. This picture was taken about two and a half weeks before the flood. (Photo courtesy Google Earth)

This picture was taken at 10:17 Monday morning. The water was still level with the floor inside the house. The water pushed the railing of the deck completely through the wall. (Photo courtesy of Drew Germain)

The bottom of the first step should be flush with the ground. The concrete that anchors some of the porch posts was pulled out of the ground on the right of the picture. (Photo by Owen Grimenstein)

This china cabinet ended up on its back, yet the stemware from our wedding came to rest in the upright position. (Photo by Owen Grimenstein)

This picture was taken with Drew's phone Monday morning. The humidity in the house fogged up his lens. The water current left the house in disarray. The couch only moved a couple of feet but the armoire had moved about ten feet from the dining room. (Photo courtesy Drew Germain)

This picture taken Monday morning shows that the bed floated, causing many items that were stacked on top of it to fall off. The bed and the bedside table came to rest against the wall just off the picture on the right, the leg of the bed puncturing the softened drywall. (Photo courtesy of Drew Germain)

The fridge floated, cabinets opened, and trash cans emptied trash all over the house. On the bottom right of this picture you can see the contrasting color of the countertops before the flood and the film of dirt the water left as it receded. (Photo by Owen Grimenstein)

The swirling waters completely rearranged this furniture. The rocking chair and dressers came to rest at almost a complete 180-degree turn from where they started in the room. (Photo by Owen Grimenstein)

The dirty residue left behind from the floodwaters. The DVDs and book floated from another room of the house before coming to rest here in the guest bathroom. (Photo by Owen Grimenstein)

One of the walls that bubbled and swelled.
(Photo by Owen Grimenstein)

The paper on the drywall bubbled and peeled.
(Photo by Owen Grimenstein)

Wooden furniture warped, swelled, or peeled.
(Photo by Owen Grimenstein)

A wicker chair in this tree and the mud line on the magnolia tree behind it show about how high the water was in the backyard. (Photo by Owen Grimenstein)

III.

Recovery

"Everywhere we went today, we saw people volunteering, church groups and neighbors helping others clean up and dry out . . . It's horrific to see what we have been seeing, but it's amazing to see the volunteers that have come out . . . I've never seen anything like it."

—*Anderson Cooper, CNN*[18]

11

Tuesday, May 4, 2010

Tuesday was Patrick's first birthday. I got up before he awoke and risked waking him up by going in to kiss him. I knew it would be a long day, and it upset me to know I was going to miss being with him on his first birthday. Allison stayed behind in Mt. Juliet to be with Patrick so we wouldn't both miss his birthday, and I left to see what I could do at the house.

Driving down Beech Bend approaching my house, I was scared. I had already seen inside the house but still wasn't sure what to expect. The now receded water would reveal a clearer picture of the devastating damage. Also, after watching footage of Hurricane Katrina in 2005 and the subsequent flooding in the Gulf of Mexico, I assumed I was going to be on my own. I didn't have a clue what to do first or how to do it. My handyman skills were limited. Would I need a permit to demo my own house after something like this? What should I demo, and how would I know what was salvageable?

I approached the house a little after 8:00 a.m., about twenty-four hours after the river reached its peak and started to recede. My dad was walking from the house to his truck. He and his brother Ed had arrived shortly before and were waiting on me. I immediately felt some relief that Dad was there; he would be able to help me organize what needed to be done. I don't think he'd ever been through anything like this either, but there was still some comfort that he would be able to help solve some of my problems for the day.

As I pulled into the driveway, the only thing that looked different about the house was that the mailbox was missing. There was no obvious damage to the front of the house, which seemed odd since I knew the damage was going to be significant. I wasn't expecting it to look like a tornado had come through, but seeing the house intact, except for the broken windows and damage from the deck in the back, brought back a resurgence of the denial I'd felt the day before when I still held out hope that my house may have only suffered minor damages.

The three of us walked around the house and property to get a better sense of the damage. Uncle Ed took as much video as he could and we began trying to give ballpark prices for how much we had paid for some of the more expensive items we'd lost in case that information was needed later. With no power for more than a day, the smoke detector was beeping away the last of its backup battery's life. Dad dismantled it, no longer worried about the risk of not having a working smoke detector.

Ed went through the house taking video of photo albums and pictures on the wall, of the now brown counter tops and floors. He looked at the bubbles in the drywall and the broken glass where the back deck went through Patrick's bedroom window. On the video, you can clearly see trash, clothes, and furniture spread out everywhere.

We couldn't get to the garage because the fridge was in the way, so Dad had to climb on top of the kitchen counter and kick the fridge back to a standing position. It landed with a loud bang that shook the house. I considered the damage that bang could do to the hardwood floor, but it was more out of curiosity than of worry. I already knew at this point that worrying about hurting the floor was laughable.

We made some preliminary decisions on where we would put the trash pile and where we would put the keep pile, along with what needed to go out first. My dad was confident that many people would come out to help and I would need to be ready to take charge and delegate. I agreed and asked him what we should do first.

For the first hour or so, the neighborhood looked normal. The birds were chirping and singing on this beautiful, sunny day. There was little traffic and very little activity. One of my neighbors had gotten an early start and had a lot of furniture already sitting in his front yard. Otherwise, no one else appeared to have gotten started.

I spoke with Jonathan briefly and he told me that FEMA had gone around earlier that morning telling everyone that black mold starts to grow within twenty-four to thirty-six hours after the water begins to recede. It seemed I was already running out of time and we hadn't even started yet.

This was overwhelming to me. I had no idea what I was supposed to do, how I would do it all in such a short amount of time, and where to even start. Thankfully, my dad quickly took over organizing everything for me because I was mentally paralyzed. He worked long hours for many days with few breaks.

I received so many calls from people wanting to help, and soon I had more than twenty people at the house working. I stayed outside a good portion of the day as people brought stuff out to me and I told them "trash" or "keep." Almost all of the salvage pile would end up in the trash pile by the end of the day. Furniture could not be saved because drawers wouldn't open and some pieces were no longer sturdy due to the swelling or warping of the wood. Most of it was too damaged to repair.

One of the first things my dad did when he found our University of Tennessee flag early Tuesday morning was hang it up on the front of the house. He wanted to make sure that Allison could see it when she got there, thinking it might help cheer her up, if only a little bit.

I learned pretty quickly that the structure sitting on Jonathan and Rebecca's front lawn was our neighbor's back deck. Somehow it got pulled out of the ground like ours did. The only difference was that the bolts that attached it to the house either didn't hold or were never there. And so it traveled around their house, across the street, and came to rest in between two trees in Jonathan and Rebecca's front yard. Those two trees probably stopped the deck from smashing into their house. One thing I had done when I rebuilt my deck was reinforce the bolts attaching the deck to the house, saving my deck from possibly the same fate.

When people first showed up to help, the looks on their faces were usually of shock and sympathy. Although some shed tears when they first arrived, the atmosphere stayed mostly positive. We tried to keep it light, even joking around a little bit when it was appropriate, like when I got onto someone for littering in my yard when he threw a sandwich wrapper on top of the growing pile of trash.

Though I didn't participate in much of those light-hearted conversations, I welcomed them because it helped me not go too deep into self-pity, and it got my mind in a better place while we worked.

As soon as I had time to think, I focused on the reality of what was around me. Even when the conversations were light, I remained in a constant state of anxiety. I could feel the uneasiness in my stomach and chest and the mental fatigue; it reminded me of how I felt in college after staying up all night to study for a final exam. I've never had a panic attack but for the first couple of days after the flood, I felt like I was constantly on the verge of having one.

In Patrick's bedroom closet we had kept shelves of clothes that Patrick would grow into and several boxes of diapers. They had become so heavy with the weight of the water that when the water receded, the shelves broke or tore from the soggy wall. This made one large heap on the floor and left holes where the shelves had been attached to the drywall. The floor was covered in—now useless—clothes that he would never wear and diapers by the hundreds that were now swelled to twice their size and much more than that in weight.

Seeing baby toys and furniture scattered throughout the house as the day went on, it was hard to imagine that a baby once loved those toys. Some of them helped Patrick sleep, some calmed him down, and some made him giggle. Two days before, they had been covered in baby drool; now they were covered in river mud. The flood had tossed these items around with complete disregard of what they meant to us. Stepping on broken glass where our baby played, seeing a once-clean crib sheet in a crib that was now brown and dripping smelly water, walking on muddy carpet where we didn't allow the dogs, and seeing Patrick's room in disarray were all hard to take. A few people started to tear up when they were in his room, though they tried not to let me see.

My next-door neighbors Luke and Callie have a daughter the same age as Patrick. Luke described the same experience at his house: "In one neighborhood west of downtown, residents scoured through debris, trying to determine how much they've lost. Luke Oakman finally got a look at the room he and his wife designed for their 11-month-old daughter after the family fled their home on Sunday. It was ruined. Baby toys and books sat on a mud-coated floor and a wooden bed leaned back against a wall. A rocking chair was propped up by the child's dresser that had been knocked over. 'I broke down when I saw that,' the 32-year-old lab worker said."[19]

I tried not to cry in front of everyone. There were enough people around that I was self-conscious, even though I knew no one would have judged me. I also didn't want to cry for myself, thinking, *This isn't the time . . . not yet.* I felt it coming many times but distracted myself. My voice certainly cracked and I teared up on occasion, but I was able to hold it together for most of the day.

As I looked around throughout that first day, there were police cars, helicopters, and FEMA trucks swarming the neighborhood. Some people were walking up and down the streets wearing face masks like they needed to be protected from biological weapons or like we were in the middle of a pandemic. It felt like I was at the epicenter of a terrorist attack or earthquake. Regardless of which analogy you use, the one I thought about the most was a war zone. What a cliché, but that is exactly what it felt like, especially once the debris from inside the houses began to pile up in the yards. It's like when people repeatedly describe a tornado by comparing the sound to a freight train. There is a reason everyone uses that comparison—it's accurate.

As the day progressed I saw evidence of the sheer power of the water. So strong yet so unpredictable. People lost sheds that they would never find. One neighbor gained a shed and no one knew who it had belonged to. How far had it traveled? We lost a plastic playground set and a nice, heavy, handmade wooden swing that disappeared down the river. A good section of our fence was also gone.

Jonathan's shed that we got everything out of the night before the flood had disappeared, but a small wooden bench that had been sitting twenty feet away hadn't moved an inch. They later found their shed on an informational brochure for the Harpeth River Watershed Association, who would be cleaning up the riverbanks for months after the flood.

The water bent our garage door inward, and the water current in the garage, along with faulty craftsmanship by the original builders, caused a crack in our home's foundation that extended from wall to wall. The wall with the foundation crack was visibly bowed outward at the bottom, making it look unstable.

I found our mailbox across the street against a fence. It had been pushed against it and when the fence held strong and the water receded, it, too, lowered to the ground. I walked it back to its hole and stuck the post back in. It made me feel a little better that people could find my house more easily. Jonathan never did find his mailbox.

Later in the day, Carrie watched Patrick and Allison made her first trek out to our home since the evacuation. It was very hard for her to see the house that first time. She took a few minutes to weep and look around. At first, she tried to save things off the trash pile. She picked up a blanket that was hers as a child. Crying, she tried to wipe off the blanket that was now stained brown and still dripping water before giving up and putting it back on the pile. She did this several times as if saying good-bye to these possessions. After her initial emotional reaction of seeing the house, Allison joined me in the front yard to sort through the piles of stuff to keep and stuff to trash.

I remember Dad pulling Allison to the side and telling her that the crib wasn't going to fit through the doors and he wanted to make sure it was okay to break it apart, warning her that he was going to have to use a sledgehammer and it would be loud. He knew it would be upsetting. We both stayed outside in the front yard but the sound traveled to us easily. Allison and I both remember the loud sound of the sledgehammer coming down on the crib, banging, cracking, popping. It was hard to listen to. Allison cried and we both flinched or shut our eyes with each blow, wishing it would all just go away, until the sound finally stopped and the pieces started to come out of the house one at a time to be thrown onto the pile. To her, this was a loss of something that represented the safety and security of our home, and its destruction in such a violent way became one of her most poignant memories of that time. My mom had come to the house by this point, and she provided Allison another shoulder to cry on.

After everything was out of the house, we began ripping out the drywall. We cut it about six inches above where the water line was, and several people, including my brother-in-law Jason, took turns taking it out of the house using wheelbarrows. Someone put a piece of plywood on the front steps to use as a ramp. This was a great idea and worked wonderfully for a few minutes, but the people using the wheelbarrows had muddy shoes, making the wood more and more slippery as the day wore on.

My mom didn't realize the ramp was slippery and went to walk up it. She fell off the ramp and into the bushes, hurting her leg. I'm sure it hurt a lot worse than she let on. She wasn't the only one who fell; there were several times that someone fell on his backside or just slid down the ramp like it was a sheet of ice while still holding on to the wheelbarrow. It became so dangerous that most people started using the steps to the side of the wood to walk down while still using the ramp for the wheelbarrow. This was awkward and humorous and caused more accidental wheelbarrow spills.

So many people came out to help that I turned some people away. One of my neighbors had recently lost her son tragically. One man that I went to church with, Vince, showed up at my door wanting to help. I looked around and there were so many people working that I couldn't think of one productive thing for him to do. Then I thought of my neighbor and how I couldn't possibly understand what she was going through. I asked him to go over there and make sure she was taken care of. He did and would later tell me that one of his more lasting images of the days following the flood was seeing her sitting on her driveway spreading out pictures to dry. He said she seemed to move around in slow motion, as if in shock.

At some point in the afternoon, I came across a desk drawer that had several tapes in it from our video camera. These included our only video copies of our honeymoon, my college mission trips, some videos of Patrick when he was an infant, and several Christmases and other family gatherings. I sat on the ground out in the front yard—with my destroyed home behind me, a giant pile of my possessions in front of me, helicopters flying above me, people walking around me with face masks on, police cars with their sirens on, and FEMA emergency trucks driving around like it was a war zone— holding physical evidence of some of the most treasured

90

moments in our lives, now erased. I sat on the grass, covered my face, and sobbed. It was Allison's turn to comfort me. I saw Luke look over at me and I didn't care that he saw me. I heard him say, "You okay?" in a way that told me he understood. I couldn't speak so I just nodded my head.

I was aware of the people walking around me and the awkward silence that they now worked in while I was visibly upset in front of them, but I no longer cared. Allison was with me and rubbed my back and tried to assure me that it was somehow going to be okay. It felt good to finally let those tears out. After a couple of minutes, I was able to get it together and continue working. After a long and emotional morning and afternoon, I went on to work throughout the evening and well into the night.

By the end of the day on Tuesday, everything had been taken out of the house and the drywall removed. I stood on one end of my house and could see the far wall on the opposite side of the house through the studs.

I left early enough so I would still be able to see Patrick on his birthday. I felt bad leaving the house with so much work to do but I couldn't justify missing all of his big day. On my way home my mind was on the house, thinking of nothing more than what was left to do, what we had lost, and what our future held.

I arrived at Drew and Carrie's a little after dark and was able to get cleaned up in time to help put Patrick to bed. I sat him in my lap, as I would do many more times that summer, and held him close as I read him our favorite book, *Goodnight Moon*. When we were finished reading he put his head against my chest and we cuddled in silence. Emotionally and

91

physically exhausted, I listened to the peace and quiet of his slow and heavy breathing and nothing else. I was clean and exhausted. Thoughts of the previous three days finally caught up with me, and I let myself cry quietly and kissed the back of Patrick's head.

12

Wednesday, May 5, 2010

On Wednesday we cleaned up leftover debris from crumpled drywall. Volunteers took down cabinets and my back deck. We pulled up the carpet and pried up the beautiful hardwood floors, keeping the subfloors intact, hoping to not have to replace them. I was prepared for another long day of physical work and emotional strain.

I continued to sort through stuff in the front yard when I had the chance. The ground was mostly dry and I could clearly see where the water had covered any plant life. There was a dirty film over anything that was green. Sitting in the front yard, I could smell the dirt as if I wasn't sitting on grass at all, but on the riverbank. The crape myrtle in the backyard that Drew and I swam over two days before was so covered in dirt that we couldn't tell if it had any green still on it.

Just about anywhere I went that was near a flooded area had a certain smell to it. My friend Joe said that he could smell it when he got to a certain point driving into Bellevue. He said it was like hitting a wall and he knew he was close. Mixed in with the smell of mud or dirt, I could usually smell fish, motor oil, and rotting organic matter.

The highlight of my day, and possibly my week, was when my next-door neighbor Dave called me over to the pile on his yard and said, "I've got a present for you." He had a large and guilty smile on his face that made me wonder what he was up to.

Dave and Catherine had only lived in their house for a few months. Dave and I were getting to know each other better by frequently discussing how to get rid of the moles that were constantly tearing up our yards. The methods of mole removal didn't usually include a happily-ever-after ending for the relentless animals.

Because of these moles, each time before I mowed the grass, I had to walk the entire front yard and stomp on their mounds so the ground would be flat. These trails would often leave dead patches of grass which ruined my pursuit of the perfect front lawn. The yard usually looked pretty good to everyone else, I think, but to me it stood out like a mustard stain on a white dress shirt.

Not long before the flood, Dave and I had agreed to meet at his house at dawn to strategize Armageddon for these moles. We planned to sit on his front porch and wait. We figured when we saw the creatures digging their tunnels we could kill them using some kind of spear-like tool that he had. I'm not sure if I ever would have been able to do that, but we never got a chance to try.

When I got closer, he pointed to his pile. He just kept smiling and waited for me to see it. After a few seconds of wondering why I was staring at his pile and thinking that I could be staring at my own pile, I saw what he wanted to show me.

On a piece of plywood that was leaning up against the pile I saw where he had strategically thrown a dead mole. I tapped my plastic bottle of water against his bottle of Gatorade in an impromptu moment of cheers. This provided a little happy spot in my day to know I wouldn't have to deal with them again. He had seen one or two more dead moles, but we assumed the rest must have died underground or gotten washed downriver.

Fortunately, not all animal stories that I heard involved death. I spoke with another neighbor of ours, Chad. He and his wife, Sara, lived a few doors down from us. They had left their dog, Desmond, home with a trusted dog sitter while they were out of town. He said that when the flood began on Sunday, the sitter desperately tried to get to the house, but all the routes were either unsafe, closed, or had traffic jams that prevented her from reaching Desmond in time.

By that afternoon they knew the water had entered the house, so they assumed the worst. Chad told her that she needed to get to her own home safely and not put herself in danger. She was in tears at the thought of leaving Desmond behind like that.

When Chad and Sara finally got home on Monday they were terrified of what they would find. Fortunately, instead of opening the door to heartache, they found Desmond sitting on his favorite spot on their sofa, which had floated from one end of the living room to the other. Desmond gave them a worried look as though he had made the mess himself and was going to get in trouble. In Chad's words, it looked as if Desmond was saying, "Look man, before you say anything, I want you to know I had nothing to do with this." Desmond's fur was matted and he smelled like you would expect a dog to smell after swimming in dirty water all day.

Chad assumed that Desmond had survived by standing on the sofa or other floating furniture for as many as twenty-four hours. He said that he must have also done a lot of swimming, too, because when they got him to the hotel where they stayed after the flood, he was too exhausted to jump up on the bed. Other than exhaustion, this dog, who has his own story to tell, was healthy and unharmed.

My brother, Adam, stayed and worked with me this day, long after everyone else had left, pulling the soaking wet insulation from under the house. I felt bad because he was going in to work the next morning, but he insisted on finishing the job. At that point, we thought there was a chance we would be able to save the subfloors and were trying not to pull them up. Armed with only two flashlights, we spent hours in the crawl space on our hands and knees in the mud, in the dark, with the insulation splattering and dripping all over us.

We worked together to throw handfuls of wet insulation, which was heavy and falling apart, into big piles and then throw those piles into other piles to get them closer to an exit, such as the crawl space door or the one hole that we made through the subfloor. Some of it we could throw ahead of us. An armload of it was heavy and we were limited on our hands and knees, so we couldn't throw it more than a few feet. It would often splash back at us, and contaminated water splashed me in the eyes and mouth on numerous occasions. It was grainy and I felt it crunch between my teeth until I washed it out with fresh water later. When getting the insulation out through the hole in the floor, one person could pass a small handful of the insulation up to the other person so he could put it in a wheelbarrow and wheel it outside. Every time I lifted it through the hole like that, water would run down my arm and into my shirt.

Adam stayed until close to midnight. We had finished the job and gotten all of the insulation from under the house. Before he left we embraced and I told him how much I appreciated his help, though I couldn't really communicate the extent of just how much it meant to me.

Later that night, the neighborhood slept. Everything was dark around the house. No one was working at any of the houses near me, and there was no power so there were no porch lights or street lights. It was a strange feeling—like I was standing in the middle of an abandoned town. The sounds of generators from distant houses were amplified through the otherwise silent night. I felt alone and vulnerable.

I got ready to go home, closing the doors and windows to make it look less inviting to people searching for a place that would be easy to get into. If they were going to break in and try to steal something or vandalize my house, I was going to make them work for it. I also had to bring in cleaning supplies and tables and chairs that we were using during the day so they wouldn't disappear overnight. This became a ritual I did every night before leaving.

This night, I was bringing in the tools that were still drying on the driveway, using a headlamp to see what I was doing. I was dreading the long drive out to Drew and Carrie's house in Mt. Juliet, and the thought occurred to me to just sleep in my car until morning. I felt too tired to drive, plus I would much rather use that forty-five minutes in a more productive way, like cleaning or sleeping. But I wanted and needed to see my family.

I was in my own little world thinking about the recent events when a police officer came around the house and shined his flashlight in my face. "Can I see your ID please?" he calmly asked me at the same time he appeared around the corner. I hadn't heard him coming so I jumped. For a split second I thought it might be someone I didn't want sneaking up on me in the middle of the night; however, I figured out pretty quick, through the bright beam, that it was a police officer. "You scared me to death, sir," I said with a smile, purposely keeping my hands visible. For the second time in two days, I was having to show my ID to prove I belonged in my own neighborhood.

He lowered the flashlight away from my face and I could see that he was remaining at the corner of the house, partially behind the wall, still ready to run for cover if he needed to. Keeping his hand on the gun on his belt, he said, "What are you doing out here tonight?" His voice was inquisitive and friendly, but his posture was ready for a fight. I gave him my driver's license and said, "This is my house and I'm just cleaning up before I leave for the night." He saw what he needed to see on my license, relaxed his hand away from the gun, and handed my license back to me. He said, "This is all crazy isn't it?"

We talked about the flood and I asked him if there had been much looting. "Nothing in this neighborhood, but there've been a few calls in other areas. Nothing like we thought it'd be though." I asked him how long they were going to be patrolling and he said, "All night long for at least a few weeks, I'm sure." I asked him how often he got around to my house and he replied, "It looks like I am making a loop about every twelve minutes or so."

He told me he had seen my headlamp shining through the house on one of his passes and snuck around back to make sure I wasn't someone that wasn't supposed to be there. I thanked him for taking it seriously and for acting on what he saw. After talking for a few more minutes, he said, "Gotta get back to it." I told him to be careful and went back to work. I saw him driving past my house two more times that night before I left.

Allison's mom and dad had come in from Memphis that day. When I went inside Drew and Carrie's house, Allison's mom greeted me at the door and gave me a big hug and kiss on the cheek and walked away. Her eyes were watering and she said nothing. This was the first time she had kissed me since our wedding five years before. Smiling, Allison said, "She's glad you got her daughter and grandson out of the house." I have no doubt that Allison would have gotten herself and Patrick out safely, but it was a nice thought. I know she was just glad we were all safe.

13

Clean-Up

For the first couple of days after the water receded, there was a constant traffic jam on our road, which was so packed that police were riding by on bicycles. Eventually, police put up roadblocks around the neighborhood so non-residents couldn't get in easily and so emergency vehicles could.

We would frequently see people driving by with cameras pointing out their windows. This happened so frequently, in fact, that people started putting up signs in their front yards telling those people to stop and help. We weren't just a YouTube video. Other signs starting popping up as well that were humorous and thankful.

The pile of trash got so high in our yard that I could barely see my house from the road. I could sit in a chair in my yard and not see the houses across the street.

We did finally end up adding the subfloors to the pile of trash; it would have been another place to grow mold. This just made the pile even higher. When it was at its highest I climbed it, paying close attention to the exposed nails, glass, and sharp metal. When I reached the top I stuck a long piece of wood into it like an explorer claiming new land. The piece of wood had a nail on the end and I stuck an orange piece of cloth the size of a hand towel on it so it looked like a flag. I did, of course, cut myself on some nails, but it was well worth it. This cheered Allison up, because she is a big University of Tennessee fan.

Days after everything was out of the house, I sat next to my dad in a pair of folding chairs on the front lawn and we watched a big truck pick up my stuff with a crane. Each robotic armload dropped my belongings in the back of the truck with a bang. My instincts were to ask them to be gentler because they were going to break something. It was hard to watch the things that we had cherished for so long get thrown into a giant dump truck, but it only got worse when the crane went up into the air and slammed down on it to smash and flatten everything in order to fit more. I could hear the splintering and popping of wood and shattering of glass. Each piece of sturdy furniture and article of clothing, each favorite book and toy, each dresser and bed that once had its own specific purpose was now nothing but the splintered and dirty remains of a comfortable home. I realized it was all permanently gone. What were previously my treasures were now nothing but trash on its way to its final resting place among plastic bags, fast-food wrappers, and dirty diapers. I would never see them again.

After the trucks picked up the debris from people's yards, they took it to a parking lot in Edwin Warner Park, a central temporary location the trucks went to unload the debris. This saved time and gas so they didn't have to drive to and from the dumps, where the stuff would eventually end up. Other, bigger trucks worked at this site, taking this debris to its ultimate resting grounds. Overall, they removed an estimated 111,000 tons of debris.[20] This is heavier than a fully loaded US Navy Nimitz Class aircraft carrier, the world's largest warships ever built.[21]

14

Human Empathy

People can be at their greatest when others are in their greatest need. Others spent so much of their free time and hard-earned money on the people who were in need of it the most. I was deeply humbled by the generosity of strangers, family, and friends.

In the two days immediately following the flood, volunteers—including friends, family, and strangers—had gotten everything out of my house and stripped it of all its walls and floors. This included tearing down my back deck that I was so proud of. With the help of Joe, Jonathan, and my dad, it had taken me a couple of weeks to rebuild it and only an hour or two to completely tear it down. After it was taken down, I jokingly apologized to Jonathan for not inviting him over to help tear it down again.

For a couple of weeks after the flood, I traveled around Nashville collecting items that we needed. I went to Baptist, Church of Christ, Catholic, and Methodist churches, as well as a Jewish Synagogue and a community center. Catholic Charities possibly had the greatest number of donations and stayed open for many months after the flood, long after many organizations had to move on. I found clothes that fit and were in great condition, along with toiletries, books, and toys.

One church, St. Matthew Catholic Church, gave like I was one of their own. A man who was a parishioner at St. Matthew was working at their donation site helping victims pick up items they needed. He invited me to his house and gave me a dry-cleaned sports jacket, ties, dress shirts and pants, and three pairs of gently worn dress shoes that retail for eighty dollars a pair and were still in their boxes.

People from every school that I had worked in up to this point donated household items and took up collections of money to give to me. The school that I was transferring to the next year even took up a collection, though most of them didn't even know me. So many people supported us.

In the days and weeks following the flood, busloads of people came and went, including numerous volunteers who went from house to house doing physical labor. One group of volunteers worked with us for over four hours. I felt bad they were giving up their days to do this, so I told them I didn't have anything else for them to do and sent them home. Later I looked next door and saw them working there. They had no intention of going home. They had left me and went to work for several more hours with other people.

Everyone who came to the house had a job and everyone stayed busy. If I couldn't think of anything for them to do and my dad was too busy to ask, people would just pick something up and start working. No one just sat around and did nothing. Every job was important to me and I was very aware of how dedicated everyone was to helping out.

A couple of ladies who came out to help told me they couldn't do a lot of the physical labor but wanted to help in some way, and so they helped clean the mud off of some of the tools that

103

I was trying to salvage, many of which I am still able to use today. They worked for several hours just sitting or standing in one spot and using donated Clorox wipes and paper towels to wipe down tools.

One man was slowly driving down the road asking people if they needed clothing. I stopped him because, at the time, I needed a pair of shoes. He got out of his car and walked to his trunk. He lived up the street and did not get flooded and had literally emptied his closet. He gave me some clothes that I could fit into and a pair of shoes. I expressed how humbled I was at how he was giving up all of his clothes. He shrugged and replied with a simple, "I can buy more," and continued driving to see who else needed clothes.

People walked the streets giving away food and drinks. Some went to the grocery store and bought cookies and handed them out boxes at a time. My sister, Melea, and sister-in-law, Lisa, took their young boys door-to-door and handed out homemade lemonade and sweet tea to homeowners and volunteers. This was a recurring theme for days after the flood. There was so much giving that we would occasionally have to turn food away. If we weren't paying attention or were not at the house, cases of bottled water would pile up on the front yard.

One woman, Penny Langston, gave my family a rental property in Nashville to live in that she wasn't using at the time. Instead of renting it out and making a profit, like she was planning to do, she wanted to donate it to someone who needed it. She went to church with my grandmother, who spoke up when Penny said she wanted to help. Just to be clear and so she would know what to expect, I told her we might need it for as long as a year. She genuinely didn't care. She didn't expect us to make improvements on the house or make any rent payments.

I had never been on the receiving end of such charitable donations. Yes, I've given some small amounts of money here and there to charities and to church. I've been on several mission trips to help orphans and people who are less fortunate than I am. But I have never been in a situation where I needed as much help as I did the spring and summer of 2010.

In the days and years following the flood, more than 29,000 volunteers gave more than 375,000 service hours to recovery and rebuilding efforts.[22] People were donating clothes and household items by the trashbag load. We received enough money and gift cards to help us replace a small portion of the stuff that was lost.

Years after the flood, I talked to Vince, my church friend who had helped my grieving neighbor, about what it was like to be a volunteer during this time. He was truthful when he said, "Getting motivated to start doing a community service project can sometimes be hard but this was different. This was my community and my friends. The problem wasn't getting started; it was stopping. It was hard to leave these people in need and go home to my family, knowing there was still a lot more work to do."

One term that continued to come up over and over about people who were volunteering their time was survivor's guilt. Seeing their neighbors in pain, many had a compelling need to help. What if it had been them? What if it had been you?

15

Effects of the Flood

In the days immediately following the flood, I witnessed the
many ways in which people grieve. When I got a chance to
slow down and take a minute for myself to breathe and think,
I looked around and watched the piles in front of the houses
get larger and larger. I was seeing inside people's lives—their
clothes, furniture, decorations, pictures, and art. These were
possessions that defined how people lived and showed their
personalities and beliefs. They were things that you would
only see if you were invited into their homes. I saw neighbors
crying and being embraced by whoever was nearest to them,
family and strangers.

I was now living in a surreal world. It felt like I was living
someone else's life. It was a depressing and anxious feeling
that I've only felt on drastically smaller scales. I was looking at
my stuff in the front yard, thinking, *Why is this so hard? It is
only stuff.* How could I explain this to people and to myself?
Try to look at it this way. If you look around your living room
and find a piece of furniture, you might say, "I could replace
that if I need to. It isn't that big of a deal. It wouldn't be the
end of the world." You are right; I would have done the same
thing. But this was different. It wasn't that I was just going to
have to replace a few things. Some of our stuff didn't just
break. Just about everything we owned was taken suddenly.
This stuff, as a whole, helped define us. This is what we called

home and what made us feel comfortable and secure. Losing it like this made us feel vulnerable, violated, and wounded. I felt defeated.

Allison and I certainly carried our stress differently. She would see something in the mud or on the trash pile and start crying. These were hand-stitched blankets from family members from long ago, baby toys, antique furniture that was handed down to us, a book that was written by her late godfather that had a personal note to her in it, and other possessions that had immeasurable sentimental value we would not be able to pass down to our kids.

I, however, kept myself busy and mostly internalized my grief. I obsessed over working at the house. After the house was gutted and everything remained on the front yard waiting to be taken away, there was nothing to do but wait. Wait for the banks, wait to find a new house, and—after we decided not to remain in our flooded home—wait for potential buyers for our flooded house.

I still went to the Beech Bend house to walk around or try to find something to do. The weeds in the front flower bed had grown and spread exponentially, another result of the river. Seeds had traveled and floated until the water was finished with them and placed them in their new homes. I watched as the weeds quickly overtook the flower bed. There were no signs of life from the daylilies that we planted months before.

I took a few long walks around the neighborhood. On these walks I saw that I wasn't alone in my grief, but still I felt like no one else could understand what we were going through.

On one of these walks I saw an RV that had come to rest balanced on top of someone's shed. I do know that this RV did not belong to the property owners where it came to rest. There was also a set of steps that once went down to the river behind Jonathan's house that now rested high above the water in the trees, an eerie reminder of the water level. There were tents that churches set up stationed around the neighborhood to give out food, cleaning supplies, and even do laundry for people. Red Cross trucks routinely drove around giving out information, food, and water. People continued to help one another recover.

16

Once Things Were Quiet

In the months following the flood, I regularly visited the house to make sure no one had been there illegally. I also wanted to walk around the house in silence, remembering the good times we had there. Before the flood, I was able to walk around the house in the dark, shoeless, not paying attention. Now, instead of walking around on my nice floors in my socks, I had to wear shoes and balance carefully on the floor joists so I wouldn't fall down into the crawl space or bump against nails that were sticking out of the wall studs.

On every visit, I went to Patrick's room and looked at the top of his wall at the clouds I had painted there that once represented peace and comfort and now looked down at the destruction below. It felt like I was saying good-bye to an old friend.

We considered ourselves lucky because we didn't lose anyone. Eleven people died in the Nashville area,[23] including one person whose body wasn't found for more than four months after the water receded.

I like to think that I am good about maintaining a positive attitude in just about every situation. However, the unintentional, self-absorbed tunnel vision that I retained after the flood was hard to overcome. I had sympathy for the families of those who died, but it, unfortunately, felt distant. Even though it was so close to home and could have just as easily been me, it was like they were a part of a natural disaster in a different part of the world.

I focused on writing down everything I could remember. I collected statistics, phone records, and pictures to document our journey and talked to other flood survivors and people who helped us rebuild to hear what they experienced. I didn't want this story to be forgotten. I wanted my kids to be able to one day read it and for Patrick to realize what he also went through and survived.

For several years after the flood, I continued to do research, watch videos, read other people's blogs and stories, and even asked people who helped what some of their memories were, thinking it would jog a memory for me. Allison and I both drove by the house when we could and watched the new owners tear down what we left and rebuild it their own way. They planted an entirely new flower bed in the front of the house and put up new siding. They took down the shrubs that lined the house along the driveway and cut down our evergreen tree but still use the same mailbox. I wondered about the new owners and what they were doing inside. Were they treating it right? I used to be able to just walk in at any time I wanted, but now I couldn't do that. Now I would be trespassing. It felt strange to have a new owner living inside. There was a small part of me that still felt like it was my house and a stranger was living there without my permission. If they knocked a hole in the wall or renovated, I felt like they needed to get my approval first.

For Allison the flood is a sad memory, particularly having the contents of our house displayed on the front yard for people to drive by and look at like lights and decorations during

Christmastime. For us both, every time it rains heavily, we still get the same anxious feeling I had while driving through the water the day before the flood, while we were packing up to leave, during the evacuation, and a good portion of the time throughout the cleanup phase. Whether it has rained recently or not, we both look down at the water every time we drive over the Harpeth River.

"What if" questions continue to haunt us. What if we had started packing as soon as Jonathan had called? Forty minutes would have given us enough time to save a lot more. What if I had stayed behind after Allison and Patrick left? That would have given me at least a couple of hours to move stuff into the attic. What if we had flood insurance? Would we still be living there today? We should have recognized the threat of getting flooded the night before. What if I had gotten a rental truck and packed all night? I could have gotten the majority of our stuff out by morning. What if I had been washed away on Highway 96 the day before evacuating, or if we had taken a left out of the driveway instead of a right when fleeing our home?

17

Buying and Selling a House

Starting with our Beech Bend house on May 1, 2010, we lived in five different places in about a year, including Drew's and Carrie's home in Mt. Juliet for about three months, my parents in Fairview for nearly a month, the rent-free rental house in Nashville for around eight months, and finally our new home.

Allison spent most of her time doing research on the many options we had regarding what to do with the house. She researched how we could keep and restore the house, how we could sell it, and the pros, cons, and costs of each option. One major factor in the decision-making process was that, like many of the homeowners around us, we didn't have flood insurance. Multiple estimates to rebuild our house were over one hundred thousand dollars, a cost steeply increased because of the foundation crack. Plus, even if we had been able to find a way to rebuild, we questioned how much peace of mind we would have living in the same house, waiting for the same thing to happen again. Rebuilding was an unlikely option.

Allison is solely responsible for doing the legwork and working with a Realtor to finally get the Beech Bend house sold fifteen months after the flood. She spent hours every day for months talking on the phone or via e-mail, ultimately making it possible for us to move forward.

During the months following the flood, we had both imagined that the day we got rid of the house would be a joyous occasion, a cause for celebration, but it was bittersweet. The process had been such a long and arduous journey and it was ending. We were now finally saying good-bye to the home we loved.

Right after we signed the paperwork, we knew that we had just closed a dark chapter in our lives and were going to begin a new one. We walked outside and hugged each other tightly. There, in the middle of the parking lot, we cried. We now had one thing that was going to allow us to write many new chapters full of happy memories, hopes, and dreams that we would carry with us the rest of our lives . . . closure. We were moving on.

Allison also did all the work that would end up getting us a new house in April of 2011, almost a year after the flood. I tell everyone that we moved down the street but up a hill. We moved to another location in Bellevue that was relatively close to where we were, but the Harpeth River never came close to getting high enough to damage it.

We didn't think the camaraderie of our old neighborhood could be replaced. It turns out that the neighborhood we moved to is different, but is just as good as the one we had to leave. The house is better, and the neighbors are just as friendly as we could have hoped.

18

Not the End

After disasters like this, humans rebuild and grow. We learn and we improve. Even our house, which was practically destroyed, was rebuilt and became a home again. Its past is now just another story diluted among hundreds of stories. Public records of this story are limited only to a footnote on a realty listing.

In the spring of 2011, not long before selling it, I went out to the house. On this particular trip I saw that one of the daylilies that we planted in the front flower bed just weeks before the flood had bloomed. This daylily had been under almost nine feet of moving water and had been neglected for over a year, but survived. Life was moving forward.

We began approaching life in a different light. We lost a lot of stuff but not the most important thing. We still had each other. What we grew to understand after the flood can be summed up with a line from a love song by Edward Sharpe and the Magnetic Zeros. We liked this song before the flood, but afterward many of the words spoke to our hearts. It is a quote that we have often talked about with each other, and I can find no other way to more appropriately close this chapter of our lives than with a message to my beautiful and patient wife: "Home is wherever I'm with you."

My neighbor's deck was torn away from their house and pushed until it got wedged in the trees in front of Jonathan's house. (Photo by Owen Grimenstein)

This is our neighbor's back deck in its final resting place on the front yard of Jonathan and Rebecca's property. This is a still shot taken from a video Ed Grimenstein took early Tuesday morning.

A still shot from the documentary *Nashville Rises*, narrated by Billy Bob Thornton. This is my next-door neighbor's deck that ended up in Jonathan's front yard. You can see our house in the top left of this shot.

Jonathan's toolshed that got washed away once sat where the cement blocks are on the left of this picture. A bench is still sitting in its original location, just on the other side of the fence on the right. (Photo by Owen Grimenstein)

Jonathan and Rebecca found this picture of their shed on a brochure for the Harpeth River Watershed Association. (Photo courtesy of the Harpeth River Watershed Association)

Missing portion of our fence (Photo by Owen Grimenstein)

The water dented our garage door inward. This is a still shot from a video Ed Grimenstein took early Tuesday morning.

A foundation crack, visible as a gap between the two levels of bricks, caused by the movement of nine feet of water inside the garage. (Photo by Owen Grimenstein)

A pile of our stuff by the road on Tuesday afternoon. (Photo by Owen Grimenstein)

You can see how high this tree was submerged from the difference in color about halfway up. (Photo by Owen Grimenstein)

Screenshot featured from the documentary *Nashville Rises*,
narrated by Billy Bob Thornton. I am on the right side of the
screen with a hat on standing next to my brother, Adam. We
are talking to my neighbors, Dave and Catherine.

Me with my brother, Adam Grimenstein, removing insulation
from the crawl space. (Photo courtesy of Adam Grimenstein)

A University of Tennessee flag I put on a post on top of the pile to try to bring in some humor. (Photo by Owen Grimenstein)

This is a temporary debris pile at Edwin Warner Park. Trucks carried debris away from people's houses and delivered it here until workers could get the debris to its final location. (Photo by Owen Grimenstein)

Joe Christy helping out.
(Photo courtesy of Adam Grimenstein)

This is an RV that came to rest balanced on top of a shed several houses down from our house. It is unclear who the RV belonged to but it did not belong to these homeowners. (Photo by Owen Grimenstein)

The waters are still high in this picture, but you can see a step ladder wedged in the trees. This ladder, which normally went down the steep slope, is resting over twenty feet above the normal water line. (Photo by Owen Grimenstein)

The inside of our house after removing the walls and subfloors. (Photo by Owen Grimenstein)

View from Patrick's room
(Photo courtesy of Adam Grimenstein)

A daylily that bloomed a year after the flood.
(Photo by Owen Grimenstein)

Afterword

If you are interested in hearing more flood stories, you can find more than one hundred fifty through the Nashville Public Library. After the flood we heard that the library, by order of Mayor Karl Dean, was undergoing the giant task of collecting the oral histories of people who were flood victims. I wanted my story to be a part of this historical event. I wanted my great-grandchildren to be able to hear my voice when they were doing research on this story or just hear my voice when they found out it was in the public domain. On July 13, 2011, my story was added to this project. They told us that the interview usually lasted around forty-five minutes. I talked for an hour and a half.

If they weren't able to help much on-site, many people were able to help in other ways. My mom took several loads of our stuff to her house and spent days, maybe weeks, cleaning it in the hopes of salvaging it. After all that work, a lot still had to be thrown away, but all that hard work helped us salvage a few things that otherwise would have been trashed. Allison's parents lived out of town but were able to help us emotionally and financially and took care of our dogs for several months while we were displaced. Tons of other friends and relatives gave more support than I can possibly measure or acknowledge.

If you helped us after the flood and I did not mention your name, then you were among the hundreds of people who

125

helped us out in a way that I am forever grateful. Many donated physical labor or material items to help us get back on track. Many others donated financially. All forms of giving were received with a wounded, but gracious heart, and what everyone did will never be forgotten.

Notes

1. U.S. Department of Commerce. "Service Assessment Record Floods of Greater Nashville: Including Flooding in Middle Tennessee and Western Kentucky, May 1-4, 2010," xi. Accessed March 25, 2016. http://www.nws.noaa.gov/os/assessments/pdfs/Tenn_Flooding.pdf.

2. Tennessee Emergency Management Agency. "May Storms and Flooding of 2010." Accessed March 25, 2016. http://www.tnema.org/events/index.html.

3. Metropolitan Government of Nashville. "Severe Flooding May 2010-After Action Report," 8. Accessed March 25, 2016. https://www.nashville.gov/Portals/0/SiteContent/OEM/docs/AARIP.pdf.

4. U.S. Army Corps of Engineers. "May 2010 Flood Event Cumberland River Basin-After Action Report," 15. Accessed March 25, 2016. https://www.hsdl.org/?view&did=21310

5. Metropolitan Government of Nashville. "Severe Flooding May 2010-After Action Report," 8. Accessed March 25, 2016. https://www.nashville.gov/Portals/0/SiteContent/OEM/docs/AARIP.pdf.

6. U.S. Army Corps of Engineers. "May 2010 Flood Event Cumberland River Basin-After Action Report," 15. Accessed March 25, 2016.

7. National Weather Service. Accessed March 26, 2016. http://www.srh.noaa.gov/ohx/?n=historicalraineventbr eaksmanynashvillerecords2.

8. Metropolitan Government of Nashville. "Severe Flooding May 2010-After Action Report," 8. Accessed March 25, 2016. https://www.nashville.gov/Portals/0/SiteContent/OEM/ docs/AARIP.pdf.

9. Ibid.

10. U.S. Army Corps of Engineers. "May 2010 Flood Event Cumberland River Basin-After Action Report," 4. Accessed March 25, 2016.

11. Metropolitan Government of Nashville. "Severe Flooding May 2010-After Action Report," 128. Accessed March 25, 2016.

12. U.S. Department of Commerce. "Service Assessment Record Floods of Greater Nashville: Including Middle Tennessee and Western Kentucky, May 1-4, 2010," xi. Accessed March 25, 2016. http://www.nws.noaa.gov/os/assessments/pdfs/Tenn_F looding.pdf.

13. Ibid., 12. Accessed March 25, 2016.

14. Metropolitan Government of Nashville. "Severe Flooding May 2010-After Action Report," 9. Accessed March 25, 2016.

15. Mayor Karl Dean, "State of Metro Address" (speech, Hume-Fogg High School, Nashville, TN, April 26, 2011).

16. Peter Miller, "Extreme Weather," NationalGeographic.com, September 2012, accessed April 24, 2016.

http://ngm.nationalgeographic.com/2012/09/extreme-weather/miller-text

17. Karen Grigsby, "20 things to know about the 2010 flood," Tennesseean.com, May 3, 2016, accessed March 26, 2016. http://www.tennessean.com/story/news/local/2015/04/30/nashville-flood-20-things-to-know/26653901/.

18. Cooper, Anderson. "Nashville Rising; Oil Spill's Environmental Impact" *Anderson Cooper 360 Degrees*. CNN. Aired May 6 2010. Transcript. http://transcripts.cnn.com/TRANSCRIPTS/1005/06/acd.01.html.

19. MSNBC.com. "Rescuers Hope for No More victims in Floods." Accessed March 25, 2016. http://www.nbcnews.com/id/36891589/ns/weather/t/rescuers-hope-no-more-victims-floods/.

20. Karen Grigsby, "20 things to know about the 2010 flood," Tennesseean.com, May 3, 2016, accessed March 26, 2016. http://www.tennessean.com/story/news/local/2015/04/30/nashville-flood-20-things-to-know/26653901/.

21. Naval-Technology.com. "The 10 Biggest Aircraft Carriers." Accessed June 12, 2016. http://www.naval-technology.com/features/feature-the-10-biggest-aircraft-carriers/.

22. Nashville.gov. "Nashville Flood May 2010." Accessed March 25, 2016. http://www.nashville.gov/Government/History-of-Metro/Nashville-Flood-May-2010.aspx.

23. U.S. Department of Commerce. "Service Assessment Record Floods of Greater Nashville: Including Middle Tennessee and Western Kentucky, May 1-4, 2010," page xi. Accessed March 25, 2016.

http://www.nws.noaa.gov/os/assessments/pdfs/Tenn_F
looding.pdf.

Acknowledgments

I should first and foremost thank my parents, Jim and Kathy Grimenstein. I think I was a relatively easy kid, but I wasn't perfect. Thank you for your patience and love. Thank you for raising me to be who I am. Mom, I really wish you could have read this. I miss you.

And thanks to Glen and Kathy Germain. I couldn't ask for better in-laws. Thanks for accepting me into your family, thanks for supporting us so much after the flood, and, most importantly, thanks for trusting me with your daughter. I hope I've done well.

Thank you, Drew and Carrie Germain, for opening your home to us. Our stay was long, but we always felt welcome and loved. Thanks for your patience and acceptance.

Thanks to my sister-in-law and proofreader extraordinaire, Lisa Grimenstein, and my editor, Natalie Haneman. Natalie, your fresh perspective on a book that has been long in the making made all the difference.

Thank you to the people of St. David's Episcopal Church. You took us in before the flood and supported us after it. You define what it means to be a church family and good servants to one another and the community.

And then there's Joe. Joe, if it weren't for you and your guidance, I think this story never would have been written. You taught me to organize my thoughts and write more about some things and less about others to help with the flow. You also came up with the title, *Under Water*. That was a good idea, by the way. I think I'll use it.

And last but not least, thank you, Allison, for being my best friend, wife, and the amazing mother of our children. Thanks for all of the free proofreading and editing and for reminding me of things to include in the book that I had nearly forgotten. I'm glad it's you I'm on this journey with.

Author's Note

Thank you so much for taking the time to read my book. I would appreciate it if you would take a minute to rate it and write a quick review on Amazon.com and Goodreads.com. Authors, especially independent ones, rely heavily on ratings and reviews for success.

If you would like to read more about the flood or behind-the-scenes details about this book, you can go to www.owengrim.wordpress.com. I included some supplementary stories, videos, and pictures that I was unable to include in the book. You can also follow me on Instagram at owengrimauthor.

Made in the USA
Charleston, SC
07 January 2017